Getting Started with Terraform

Second Edition

Manage production infrastructure as code

Kirill Shirinkin

Packt>

BIRMINGHAM - MUMBAI

Getting Started with Terraform

Second Edition

Copyright © 2017 Packt Publishing

All rights reserved. No part of this book may be reproduced, stored in a retrieval system, or transmitted in any form or by any means, without the prior written permission of the publisher, except in the case of brief quotations embedded in critical articles or reviews.

Every effort has been made in the preparation of this book to ensure the accuracy of the information presented. However, the information contained in this book is sold without warranty, either express or implied. Neither the author, nor Packt Publishing, and its dealers and distributors will be held liable for any damages caused or alleged to be caused directly or indirectly by this book.

Packt Publishing has endeavored to provide trademark information about all of the companies and products mentioned in this book by the appropriate use of capitals. However, Packt Publishing cannot guarantee the accuracy of this information.

First published: January 2017

Second edition: July 2017

Production reference: 1280717

Published by Packt Publishing Ltd.
Livery Place
35 Livery Street
Birmingham
B3 2PB, UK.

ISBN 978-1-78862-353-7

www.packtpub.com

Credits

Author
Kirill Shirinkin

Reviewer
Anton Babenko

Commissioning Editor
Kartikey Pandey

Acquisition Editor
Prachi Bisht

Content Development Editor
Trusha Shriyan

Technical Editor
Naveenkumar Jain

Copy Editor
Safis Editing

Project Coordinator
Judie Jose

Proofreader
Safis Editing

Indexer
Pratik Shirodkar

Graphics
Kirk D'Penha

Production Coordinator
Aparna Bhagat

About the Author

Kirill Shirinkin is an IT consultant who focuses on Cloud technologies and DevOps practices. He has worked in companies of different sizes and areas, from an online language learning leader to a major IT provider for the global travel industry and one of the largest management consultancies. He is also a cofounder of online mentorship platform `mkdev.me`, where he leads a team and teaches his students all about DevOps.

About the Reviewer

Anton Babenko is currently working as a senior automation engineer at Stelligent Systems AB, where he specializes in infrastructure management and deployment using Amazon Web Services. He is an AWS certified professional with all five available certifications. Also, he has been working as a web developer, team lead, and chief technology officer for the last 10 years. He has been constantly involved in automation (from testing to marketing) and exploring ways to do it properly and as risk-free as possible. He has strong interest and experience in the DevOps toolset.

www.PacktPub.com

For support files and downloads related to your book, please visit `www.PacktPub.com`.

Did you know that Packt offers eBook versions of every book published, with PDF and ePub files available? You can upgrade to the eBook version at `www.PacktPub.com` and as a print book customer, you are entitled to a discount on the eBook copy. Get in touch with us at `service@packtpub.com` for more details.

At `www.PacktPub.com`, you can also read a collection of free technical articles, sign up for a range of free newsletters and receive exclusive discounts and offers on Packt books and eBooks.

Mapt

`https://www.packtpub.com/mapt`

Get the most in-demand software skills with Mapt. Mapt gives you full access to all Packt books and video courses, as well as industry-leading tools to help you plan your personal development and advance your career.

Why subscribe?

- Fully searchable across every book published by Packt
- Copy and paste, print, and bookmark content
- On demand and accessible via a web browser

Customer Feedback

Thanks for purchasing this Packt book. At Packt, quality is at the heart of our editorial process. To help us improve, please leave us an honest review on this book's Amazon page at `link`.

If you'd like to join our team of regular reviewers, you can e-mail us at `customerreviews@packtpub.com`. We award our regular reviewers with free eBooks and videos in exchange for their valuable feedback. Help us be relentless in improving our products!

Table of Contents

Preface   1

Chapter 1: Infrastructure Automation   7
- **What is Infrastructure as Code and why is it needed?**   7
- **Declarative versus procedural tools for Infrastructure as Code**   9
- **Infrastructure as Code in the Cloud**   11
- **Requirements for infrastructure provisioner**   12
  - Supports a wide variety of services   13
  - Idempotency   13
  - Dependency resolution   13
  - Robust integration with existing tools   13
  - Platform agnosticism   14
  - Smart update management   14
  - Ease of extension   14
- **Which tools exist for infrastructure provisioning?**   14
  - Scripting   15
  - Configuration management   15
  - CloudFormation/Heat   16
  - Terraform   16
- **A short overview of Terraform**   16
- **Journey ahead and how to read this book**   17
- **Summary**   18

Chapter 2: Deploying First Server   19
- **History of Terraform**   20
- **Preparing work environment**   21
- **The many Terraform providers**   22
- **Short introduction to AWS**   23
- **Using Elastic Compute Cloud**   24
  - Creating an instance through the Management Console   25
  - Creating an instance with AWS CLI   27
- **Configuring AWS provider**   29
  - Static credentials   29
  - Environment variables   29
  - Credentials file   30
- **Creating an EC2 instance with Terraform**   30

Working with state	33
Handling resource updates	36
Destroying everything we've built	38
Summary	39

Chapter 3: Resource Dependencies and Modules — 41

Creating an AWS Virtual Private Cloud	42
Understanding dependency graph	44
Playing with Terraform graphs	46
Controlling dependencies with depends_on and ignore_changes	50
Making sense of our template	53
Removing duplication with modules	54
Configuring modules	57
Retrieving module data with outputs	60
Using root module outputs	61
Summary	62

Chapter 4: Storing and Supplying Configuration — 63

Understanding variables	63
Using map variables	65
Using list variables	67
Supplying variables inline	70
Using Terraform environment variables	71
Using variable files	72
Configuring data sources	73
Providing configuration with template_file	76
Providing data from anywhere with external_data	80
Exploring Terraform configuration resources	81
Taking a quick look at Consul	84
Summary	86

Chapter 5: Connecting with Other Tools — 87

Returning data with outputs	87
Testing servers with Inspec	88
Provisioners	92
Provisioning with local-exec and Ansible	93
Provisioning with Chef	95
Provisioning with remote-exec and Puppet	97
Uploading files with a file provisioner	99
Reprovisioning machines with null_resource	101
Using third-party plugins	103

Summary	105
Chapter 6: Scaling and Updating Infrastructure	**107**
Counting servers	108
Bringing in high availability	114
Load balancing and simulating conditionals	116
Immutable infrastructure	120
Baking images with Packer	123
Rolling out AMI upgrades with Terraform	127
Performing blue-green deployments	131
Refreshing infrastructure	137
Importing resources	138
Summary	140
Chapter 7: Collaborative Infrastructure	**143**
Version control with Git 101	144
Moving templates to Git	146
Protecting secrets in a Git repository	148
Storing state files remotely	151
Connecting remote states together	156
Storing modules remotely	161
Locking state files with Terragrunt	163
Moving infrastructure updates to the CI pipeline	167
Integration testing of Terraform modules	175
Summary	179
Chapter 8: Future of Terraform	**181**
Infrastructure as code and Terraform replacements	181
Learning AWS and compiling Terraform	182
Learning Consul	183
Provisioning and configuration management	183
Immutable infrastructure	183
Collaboration and CI/CD	184
The many tools around Terraform	185
The rapid development of Terraform	186
Closing thoughts on the future of Terraform	187
Summary	189
Index	**191**

Preface

With ever-rising adoption of Cloud technologies and infrastructure SaaS products, as well as always the constantly sizes of infrastructures the need, to manage it all in the form of code becomes more and more apparent. Cloud providers such as Amazon Web Services have dozens of services and all of them require secure, re-usable and predictable configuration. Terraform, the primary tool for this job, appeared in 2014 and quickly gained popularity among system administrators and software developers. Since the first release, Terraform has achieved a lot of traction. It became the new de facto tool for managing the cloud environments. Terraform is also a tool that is quite new, that is changing with every release and that requires a new mindset and new practices from teams that adopt it.

In this book you will learn how Terraform works and how to use it, with many examples of real-life applications of it. You will explore modern approaches to managing the infrastructure, such as Infrastructure as Code and Immutable Infrastructure. You will also learn many new small utilities that either improve the experience of working with Terraform or cover the layers that Terraform is not supposed to manage. By the end of this book not only will you now how to use Terraform, but you will be in an expert in treating your whole Infrastructure as Code, with Terraform being the core of this procedure.

What this book covers

Chapter 1, *Infrastructure Automation*, covers infrastructure automation in general, why is it needed at all (with a list of the main reasons to do it) and which tools exist to solve this problem. By the end of this chapter you will know which problem Terraform solves and why it is the best tool for particular infrastructure automation tasks.

Chapter 2, *Deploying First Server*, walks through all the necessary steps to install Terraform, gives a short overview of AWS and EC2, and explain in detail how to create your very first EC2 instance with Terraform.

Chapter 3, *Resource Dependencies and Modules*, explains one of most important features of Terraform: dependency graph. You will figure out how dependencies work and see it in practice by extending the template from previous chapter. At the moment we find out our template is too big, we will use Terraform modules to DRY our code and also use more advanced dependency features.

Preface

Chapter 4, *Storing and Supplying Configuration*, teaches how to make Terraform templates more configurable. You will see all the possible ways to supply data to Terraform templates, to basic variables to using any external data source.

Chapter 5, *Connecting with Other Tools*, talks about how you can connect Terraform templates to external tools. It shows how to combine Terraform and Ansible, Puppet, or Chef, how to provision servers, and how to run Inspec tests against them.

Chapter 6, *Scaling and Updating Infrastructure*, dives deep into managing existing infrastructures with Terraform. It gives an overview of the various ways to perform updates with Terraform and explains what Immutable Infrastructure is and how to use it with Terraform. It gives a full example of performing both rolling updates and blue-green deployments, as well as tricks on running smaller updates.

Chapter 7, *Collaborative Infrastructure*, provides best practices of using Terraform in a team. It shows how to refactor and split Terraform templates into remote modules, how to organize your code to be re-usable, and how to handle sensitive data inside Terraform templates. It also teaches how to do full Continuous Integration of a Terraform-based infrastructure.

Chapter 8, *Future of Terraform*, speculates on the future of Terraform. It also recaps everything learned so far and gives some extra thoughts and hints on topics that were too small too deserve a separate chapter.

What you need for this book

This book assumes a basic level of understanding the Linux operating system. The book will go through configuring numerous AWS resources. Being familiar with AWS is a plus, but is not required, as all required services will be explained. Usage of some cloud services in this book will require you to spend a dollar or two on them. Although the book assumes Linux as the primary workstation operating system, all of the content applies to MacOS and most of it will work the same way on Windows as well.

Internet connectivity is required to install the necessary tools, including Terraform. It is also required to perform any Terraform operations.

Who this book is for

This book is essentially intended to both software developers and system administrators, as well as specialists who have knowledge of both areas: system reliability engineers, DevOps engineers, cloud architects and so on.

Conventions

In this book, you will find a number of text styles that distinguish between different kinds of information. Here are some examples of these styles and an explanation of their meaning.

Code words in text, database table names, folder names, filenames, file extensions, pathnames, dummy URLs, user input, and Twitter handles are shown as follows: "For some reason, instead of using DNS server, you want to hardcode the IP address of this box to the /etc/hosts file with a domain name repository.internal."

A block of code is set as follows:

```
host { 'repository.internal':
  ip => '192.168.0.5',
}
```

When we wish to draw your attention to a particular part of a code block, the relevant lines or items are set in bold:

```
resource "null_resource" "app_server_provisioner" {
  triggers {
    server_id = "${join(",", aws_instance.app-server.*.id)}"
  }
  connection {
    user = "centos"
    host = "${element(aws_instance.app-server.*.public_ip, count.index)}"
  }
  provisioner "file" {
    source = "${path.module}/setup.pp"
    destination = "/tmp/setup.pp"
  }
```

Any command-line input or output is written as follows:

```
$> curl -O https://releases.hashicorp.com/terraform/0.8.2/terraform_0.8.2_linux_amd64.zip
$> sudo unzip terraform_0.8.2_linux_amd64.zip -d /usr/local/bin/
```

Preface

New terms and **important words** are shown in bold. Words that you see on the screen, for example, in menus or dialog boxes, appear in the text like this: "Click on **Launch Instance**."

> Warnings or important notes appear in a box like this.

> Tips and tricks appear like this.

Reader feedback

Feedback from our readers is always welcome. Let us know what you think about this book-what you liked or disliked. Reader feedback is important for us as it helps us develop titles that you will really get the most out of. To send us general feedback, simply e-mail feedback@packtpub.com, and mention the book's title in the subject of your message. If there is a topic that you have expertise in and you are interested in either writing or contributing to a book, see our author guide at www.packtpub.com/authors.

Customer support

Now that you are the proud owner of a Packt book, we have a number of things to help you to get the most from your purchase.

Downloading the example code

You can download the example code files for this book from your account at http://www.packtpub.com. If you purchased this book elsewhere, you can visit http://www.packtpub.com/support and register to have the files e-mailed directly to you.

You can download the code files by following these steps:

1. Log in or register to our website using your e-mail address and password.
2. Hover the mouse pointer on the **SUPPORT** tab at the top.
3. Click on **Code Downloads & Errata**.
4. Enter the name of the book in the **Search** box.

5. Select the book for which you're looking to download the code files.
6. Choose from the drop-down menu where you purchased this book from.
7. Click on **Code Download**.

Once the file is downloaded, please make sure that you unzip or extract the folder using the latest version of:

- WinRAR / 7-Zip for Windows
- Zipeg / iZip / UnRarX for Mac
- 7-Zip / PeaZip for Linux

The code bundle for the book is also hosted on GitHub at `https://github.com/PacktPublishing/Getting-Started-with-Terraform-Second-Edition`. We also have other code bundles from our rich catalog of books and videos available at `https://github.com/PacktPublishing/`. Check them out!

Downloading the color images of this book

We also provide you with a PDF file that has color images of the screenshots/diagrams used in this book. The color images will help you better understand the changes in the output. You can download this file from `https://www.packtpub.com/sites/default/files/downloads/GettingStartedwithTerraformSecondEdition_ColorImages.pdf`.

Errata

Although we have taken every care to ensure the accuracy of our content, mistakes do happen. If you find a mistake in one of our books-maybe a mistake in the text or the code-we would be grateful if you could report this to us. By doing so, you can save other readers from frustration and help us improve subsequent versions of this book. If you find any errata, please report them by visiting `http://www.packtpub.com/submit-errata`, selecting your book, clicking on the **Errata Submission Form** link, and entering the details of your errata. Once your errata are verified, your submission will be accepted and the errata will be uploaded to our website or added to any list of existing errata under the Errata section of that title.

To view the previously submitted errata, go to `https://www.packtpub.com/books/content/support` and enter the name of the book in the search field. The required information will appear under the **Errata** section.

Piracy

Piracy of copyrighted material on the Internet is an ongoing problem across all media. At Packt, we take the protection of our copyright and licenses very seriously. If you come across any illegal copies of our works in any form on the Internet, please provide us with the location address or website name immediately so that we can pursue a remedy.

Please contact us at `copyright@packtpub.com` with a link to the suspected pirated material.

We appreciate your help in protecting our authors and our ability to bring you valuable content.

Questions

If you have a problem with any aspect of this book, you can contact us at `questions@packtpub.com`, and we will do our best to address the problem.

1
Infrastructure Automation

Before starting to learn Terraform, you first need to learn certain concepts in the modern infrastructure. To be able to use the new tool, one needs to understand what problem it solves. In order to do it, this chapter will cover the following topics:

- Learning what Infrastructure as Code is and why it is needed
- Understanding the benefits of a declarative approach to configuration management
- Explaining the missing points of configuration management tools
- Laying out requirements for high-level infrastructure automation
- Taking a quick look at the main tools in order to provision infrastructure
- The short overview and history of Terraform
- What you will learn in this book

What is Infrastructure as Code and why is it needed?

The amount of servers used by almost any project is growing rapidly mostly due to increasing adoption of cloud technologies. As a result, traditional ways of managing IT infrastructure become less and less relevant.

The manual approach fits well for a farm of a dozen, perhaps even a couple of dozen of servers. But when we're talking about hundreds of them, doing anything by hand is definitely not going to play out well.

It's not only about servers, of course. Every cloud provider gives extra services on top, be it a virtual networking service, object storage, or a monitoring solution, which you don't need to maintain yourself. These services function that a **Software as a Service (SaaS)**. And actually, we should treat various SaaS products as part of our infrastructure as well. If you use **New Relic** for monitoring purposes, then it is your infrastructure too, with the difference that you don't need to manage servers for it yourself. But how you use it and whether you use it correctly is up to you.

No surprises, companies of any size, from small start-ups to huge enterprises, are adopting new techniques and tools to manage and automate their infrastructures. These techniques eventually got a new name: **Infrastructure as Code (IaC)**.

Dated something 2009, the Infrastructure as Code term is all about approaching your IT-infrastructure tasks the same way you develop software. This includes the things similar to the following:

- Heavy use of source control to store all infrastructure-related code
- Collaboration on this code in the same fashion as applications are developed
- Using unit and integration testing and even applying **Test-driven development** to infrastructure code
- Introducing continuous integration and continuous delivery to test and release infrastructure code

Infrastructure as Code is a foundation for DevOps culture because both operations and developers approach their work in the same way, and by following the principles laid out before, they already have some common ground.

This is not to say that if your infrastructure is treated as code, then the border between development and operations becomes so blurry that the whole existence of this separation can become eventually quite questionable.

Of course, the introduction of Infrastructure as Code requires new kinds of tools.

Declarative versus procedural tools for Infrastructure as Code

What is *infrastructure code* specifically? It depends highly on your particular infrastructure setup.

In the simplest case, it might be just a bunch of shell scripts and component-specific configuration files (Nginx configuration, cron jobs, and so on) stored in source control. Inside these shell scripts, you specify exact steps computer needs to take to achieve the state you need:

1. Copy this file to that folder.
2. Replace all occurrences of ADDRESS with `mysite.com`.
3. Restart the `Nginx` service.
4. Send an e-mail about successful deployment.

This is what we call procedural programming. It's not bad. For example, build steps of Continuous Integration tools such as Jenkins that are a perfect fit for a procedural approach—after all, the sequence of command is exactly what you need in this case.

However, you can only go far with shell scripts when it comes to configuring servers and higher-level pieces. The more common and mature approach these days is to use tools that provide a declarative, rather than a procedural, way to define your infrastructure. With declarative definitions, you don't need to think *how* to do something; you only write *what* should be there.

Perhaps the main benefit of it is that rerunning a declarative definition will never do the same job twice, whereas executing the same shell script will most likely break something on the second run. The proper configuration management tool will ensure that the server is in the exactly same state as defined in your code. This property of modern configuration and provisioning tools is named **idempotency**.

Let's look at an example. Let's say that you have a box in your network that hosts a packages repository. For some reason, instead of using DNS server, you want to hardcode the IP address of this box to the `/etc/hosts` file with the domain name `repository.internal`.

> In Unix-like systems, the `/etc/hosts` file contains a local text database of DNS records. The system tries to resolve the DNS name by looking at this file first, and asking DNS-server only after.

Not a complex task to do, given that you only need to add a new line to the `/etc/hosts` file. To achieve this, you could have a script like the following:

```
echo 192.168.0.5 repository.internal >> /etc/hosts/hosts
```

Running it once will do the job: required entry will be added to the end of the `/etc/hosts` file. But what will happen if you execute it again? You guessed right: exactly the same line will be appended again. And, even worse, what if the IP address of the repository box will changes? Then, if you execute your script, you will end up with two different host entries for the same domain name.

You can ensure idempotency yourself inside the script with the high usage of conditional checks. But why reinvent the wheel when there is already a tool to do exactly this job? It would be so much better to just define the end result without composing a sequence of commands to achieve this.

And that is exactly what configuration management tools such as Puppet and Chef do by providing you with a special **Domain Specific Language** (DSL) to define the desired state of the machine. The certain downside is the necessity to learn a new DSL: a special small language focused on solving one particular task. It's not a complete programming language, neither does it need to be; in this case, its only job is to describe the state of your server.

Let's look at how the same task could be done with the help of a Puppet manifest:

```
host { 'repository.internal':
  ip => '192.168.0.5',
}
```

Applying this manifest multiple times will never add extra entries, and changing the IP address in the manifest will be reflected correctly in host files, changing the existing entry and not creating a new one.

> There is an additional benefit I should mention: on top of idempotency, you often get platform agnosticism. What this means is that the same definition could be used for completely different operating systems without any change. For example, by using the *package* resource in Puppet, you don't care whether the underlying system uses `rpm` or `deb`.

Now you should better understand that, when it comes to configuration management, tools that provide the declarative way of doing things are preferred.

Modern configuration management tools such as Chef or Puppet completely solve the problem of setting up a single machine. There is an increasing number of high-quality libraries (be it cookbooks or modules) for configuring all kinds of software in an (almost) OS-agnostic way. But configuring what goes inside a single server is only part of the picture. The other part, which is located a layer above, also requires new tooling.

Infrastructure as Code in the Cloud

Quite often, servers are only one part of infrastructure. With cloud platforms such as **Amazon Web Services (AWS)**, Google Cloud Platform, and OpenStack advancing more and more, there is an increased need for automating and streamlining the way people work with the services these platforms provide. If you rely heavily on at least one cloud provider for major parts of your project, you will start meeting challenges in applying consistent patterns of their usage.

The approach of modern configuration management tools, while having been around for quite some time and having been adopted by many companies, has some inconveniences when it comes to managing anything but servers.

There is a strong likelihood you would want these patterns to be written once and then applied automatically. Even more, you need to be able to reproduce every action and test the result of it, following the aforementioned Infrastructure as Code principles. Otherwise, working with cloud providers will either end up in so-called **ClickOps**, where you work with infrastructure primarily by clicking buttons in the web interface of a cloud provider, or you will script all the processes by using APIs of this provider directly. And, even if scripting APIs sounds like a big step towards true Infrastructure as Code, you can achieve much more using existing tools for this exact task.

There is a certain need for a configuration tool that operates one level higher than a setup of a single server; a tool that would allow writing a blueprint that would define all of the high-level pieces at once: servers, cloud services, and even external SaaS products. A tool like this is called given a different name: infrastructure orchestrator, infrastructure provisioner, infrastructure templating, and so on. No matter what you call it, at some point in time, your infrastructure will really need it.

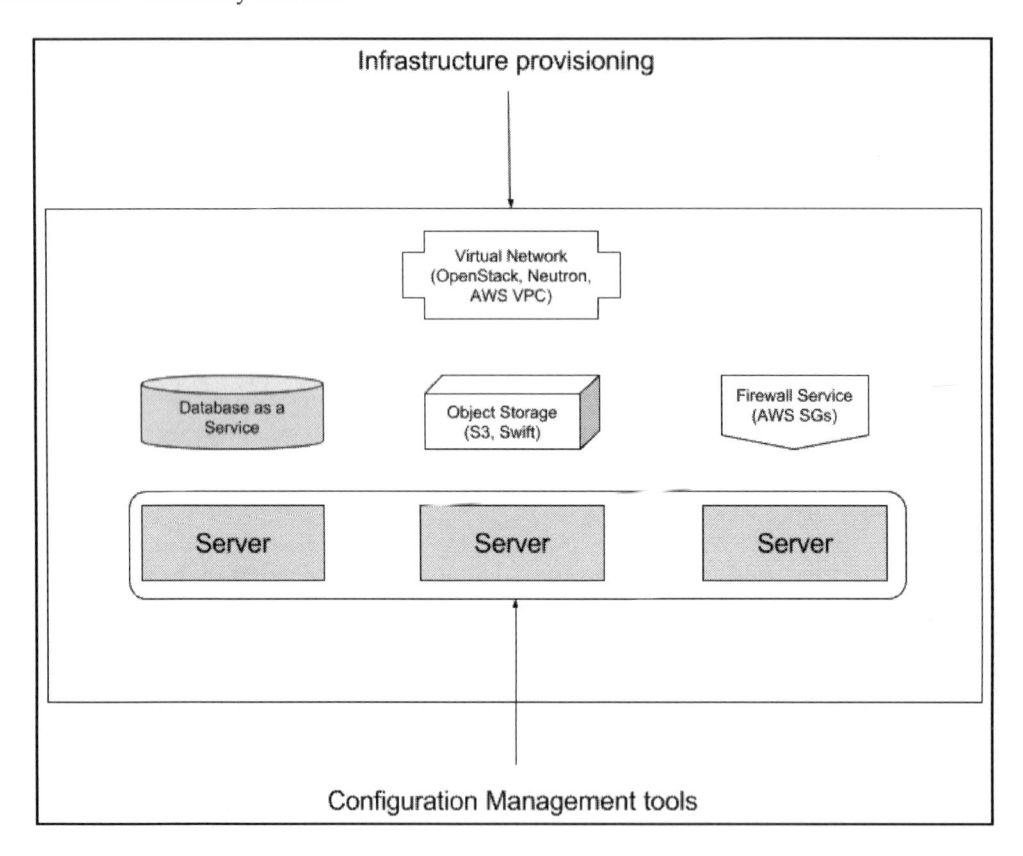

Requirements for infrastructure provisioner

Before proceeding to the existing solutions, let's lay out a list of the most important requirements for a tool such as this, so we are able to choose one wisely.

Supports a wide variety of services

AWS alone already has dozens of entities to take care of. Other players (DigitalOcean, Google Cloud, Microsoft Azure, and so on) increase this number significantly. And if you want to add smaller SaaS providers to the game, you get hundreds of resources to manage.

Idempotency

The same as with a single-server configuration, reapplying an infrastructure template should not do the job twice. If you have a template defining 50 different resources, from EC2 instances to S3 buckets, then you do not want to duplicate or recreate all of them every time you apply the template. You want only missing parts to be created, existing ones to be in the desired state, and the ones which have become obsolete to be destroyed.

Dependency resolution

It is important to be able not just to define *2 app servers, 1 DB server, and 2 security groups*, but to also point them to each other using lookup mechanism. Especially when creating a complete environment from scratch, you want to ensure the correct order of creation to achieve the flawless bootstrap of each component.

> Here, and further in the book, the term environment will mean a complete set of resources that an infrastructure consists of. It includes a network setup, all servers, and all related resources.

Robust integration with existing tools

Even though it is pretty awesome to have all infrastructures in one beautiful template, you still need to take care of what is happening on each particular server: applications need to be deployed, databases need to be configured, and so on. This is not the job for an infrastructure provisioning tool. But, certainly, a tool like this should easily integrate with other tools such as Chef, which solves this problem already.

Platform agnosticism

Ideally, templates should be platform agnostic. This means that if I define a template for *2 app servers, 1 db server, all talk to each other*, I should be able to easily switch from AWS to local Vagrant without rewriting the template. Platform agnosticism is difficult to obtain, while at the same time, might not really be needed that often. Completely changing the underlying platform is a rather rare event that happens perhaps once or twice in a product's lifetime.

Smart update management

This is a tricky one, and at the moment of writing, no tool can do it flawlessly in every case (and, honestly, it is unlikely one will ever). What happens when I change a type of three EC2 instances from `m3.medium` to `c4.xlarge`? Will my `m3.medium` instances shut down and be replaced one by one by new ones? Will they be instantly destroyed leading to a few minutes of downtime? Or will the tool, just ignore the updated instance type? Or will it not and then just override old nodes and I will end up with three new nodes and three old EC2 instances that I have to remove manually? Solutions to this problem differ from platform to platform, which makes it more complicated for the tool to be platform agnostic.

Ease of extension

The last requirement is of particular importance: there must be an easy way to extend this tool to support other resources. For example, if a tool lacks support for AWS Kinesis or a particular feature or property of already supported service, and there is no plan to support it officially, then there has to be a way to implement it yourself quickly.

Which tools exist for infrastructure provisioning?

Now that we have a problem to solve and a list of requirements the tool that should solve the problem, we can go into the specifics of the different existing tools.

Scripting

Almost every cloud provider has an API, and if there is an API, you can script it. You could also go beyond a single script and develop a small-focused tool just for your company to create environments. The disadvantages are: more software to develop and support in-house.

Configuration management

Most configuration management tools already have a way to create cloud resources. Chef has Chef provisioning, which allows you to write recipes that define, not entities on a single server, but multiple servers and components, such as security groups of AWS and networking parts. There are also Puppet modules which wrap cloud APIs into Puppet resources. Ansible also has modules to support providers, such as AWS, OpenStack, and others.

While the idea of using a single tool for both levels: high complete infrastructure definition and inside-a-server configuration, is tempting, it has some drawbacks. One of them is lack of support for many required services and the immaturity of these solutions in general.

Also, the ways to use these tools for this purpose are kind of ambiguous. There are no well-defined workflows. Let's take AWS as an example. The recommended way to set up a firewall in AWS environment is to use **security groups** (**SGs**). SGs are a separate entity, which are available via web interface or API.

What should you do if you want to create an AWS security group that allows connections from an app server to a database server? Should you put this code a database package or an application package? An AWS security group clearly doesn't belong to either of them.

The only meaningful solution is to create a separate package which is dedicated to creating the security groups and performs searches against the nodes API to define inbound and outbound rules for these groups.

It's also unclear from where to execute this kind of code. From a workstation? From a separate AWS-resources node that has permissions to do this sort of thing? How do you secure it? How do you distribute keys? And, more importantly, how do you make this process reproducible and ready to be used in CI/CD pipelines? There is no clear answer to these questions from the configuration management tools' point of view.

The other downside is that you might not even have, or want to have, a complete configuration management in your organization. Implementing them gives huge benefits, but a steep learning curve and lack of in-house expertise can be significant blockers in their adaption.

CloudFormation/Heat

Both AWS and OpenStack have a built-in way to define all of their resources in one template. Often, it works nicely in environments that are only AWS or only OpenStack. But, as soon as you want to add another provider to the mix, you need another tool.

Terraform

Finally, there is Terraform, the tool this book is about, and the one we will use to codify a complete infrastructure, or at least the top layer of it.

A short overview of Terraform

Terraform is an open source utility, created by the **HashiCorp** company, the same company that created Vagrant, Packer, Consul, and other popular infrastructure tools. It was initially released in July 2014, and since then, has come a long way to become one of the most important tools for infrastructure provisioning and management.

This is how Terraform is described by HashiCorp:

> *... a tool for safely and efficiently building, combining, and launching infrastructure. From physical servers to containers to SaaS products, Terraform is able to create and compose all the components necessary to run any service or application.* (https://www.hashicorp.com/blog/terraform.html).

Terraform easily fits most of the requirements listed here:

- At the time of writing, it supports over 30 different providers, from a huge ones such as AWS to a smaller ones such as multiple SaaS DNS providers.
- Terraform provides special configuration language to declare your infrastructure in simple text templates.
- Terraform also implements a complex graph logic, which allows you to resolve dependencies, intelligibility and reliability.

- When it comes to servers, Terraform has multiple ways of configuring and wiring them up with existing configuration management tools.
- Terraform is not platform agnostic in the sense described earlier, but it allows you to use multiple providers in a single template, and there are ways to make it somewhat platform agnostic. We will talk about these ways towards the end of the book.
- Terraform keeps track of the current state of the infrastructure it created and applies delta changes when something needs to be updated, added, or deleted. It also provides a way to import existing resources and target only specific resources.
- Terraform is easily extendable with plugins, which should be written in the Go programming language.

Over the next seven chapters, we will learn how to use Terraform and all of its features.

Journey ahead and how to read this book

This is a book about Terraform, and you will learn everything that there is to learn about this tool. There are two main parts to this book, split into six chapters of pure learning.

In the next three chapters, we will learn the basics. In `Chapter 2`, *Deploying First Server*, the next one, you will learn the basics of Terraform, the main entities it uses, and how to deploy our first server with it. We will also get a short introduction to AWS EC2.

In `Chapter 3`, *Resource Dependencies and Modules*, we will discover how exactly Terraform operates with its resources and how to refactor our code. In `Chapter 4`, *Storing and Supplying Configuration*, you will learn all the possible ways you can configure your templates with the various APIs Terraform provides.

If you are already familiar with the Terraform basics, `Chapter 2`, *Deploying First Server*, to `Chapter 4`, *Storing and Supplying Configuration*, might be a bit boring for you. They are about how to use this tool as a first-time user, and they don't cover many advanced topics that you will get to once you run Terraform in production. Feel free to skip the next three chapters if you, already used Terraform. For advanced topics, head over to `Chapter 5`, *Connecting with Other Tools*, `Chapter 6`, *Scaling and Updating Infrastructure*, and `Chapter 7`, *Collaborative Infrastructure*.

In Chapter 5, *Connecting with Other Tools*, you will learn how to connect Terraform with many different tools, from configuration management to infrastructure testing tools. We will find out how to provision and reprovision machines and how to use Terraform alongside literally any other tool.

In Chapter 6, *Scaling and Updating Infrastructure*, we will cover infrastructure updates with Terraform, from the very simple cases (such as changing one property of a non-essential resource) to complex upgrade scenarios of whole clusters of machines.

Finally, in Chapter 7, *Collaborative Infrastructure*, you will learn how to collaborate on infrastructure work with Terraform. We will also master integration testing for Terraform environments.

Be prepared: this book is not only about Terraform. It's about Infrastructure as Code and various topics surrounding it, such as **Immutable Infrastructure**. Terraform will be the main tool we study, but definitely not the only one. Configuration management tools, testing tools, half a dozen small helper utilities, and the same amount of AWS services; get ready to learn the whole toolset required to embrace Infrastructure as Code because, as you will soon notice, Terraform is a tool that must be supported by other software.

In the final chapter, Chapter 8, *Future of Terraform*, we will run through multiple topics related to Terraform which did not make it into the other chapters. That chapter, also includes a non-conventional piece on the future of Terraform, which you may or may not want to read before proceeding to learn it.

So, without further delay, let's proceed to creating our first server with Terraform.

Summary

In this chapter, you learned a lot about Infrastructure as Code principles and some tools that allow you to leverage them. There are many existing mature tools that take care of configuring what goes inside a single server, but there are not that many options when it comes to defining one level above a single server. We also listed the requirements for a tool that would take care of configuring this higher level. Then, we came to the conclusion that Terraform meets many, if not all, of these requirements. In the next chapter, we will finally get our hands dirty, install Terraform, and get to know how to use it to create a single AWS EC2 server.

2
Deploying First Server

Now that we know which problem Terraform solves, we can proceed to learning how exactly it works and how to use it. In this chapter, we will learn a bit about Terraform's history, install it on our workstation, prepare our working environment, and run the tool for the first time. After getting everything ready for our work, we will figure out what a Terraform provider is, and then we will take a quick tour of what AWS and EC2 are.

With this knowledge in place, we will first create an EC2 instance by hand (just to understand the pain that Terraform will eliminate), and then we will do exactly the same with the help of the Terraform template. That will allow us to study the nature of the Terraform `state` file. Once we know that, we will update our server using the same template, and finally, destroy it. By the end of the chapter, you will already have solid knowledge of the Terraform basics, and you will be ready to create a template for your existing infrastructure.

History of Terraform

Terraform was first released in July 2014 by a company named HashiCorp. It is the same company that brought us tool, such as Vagrant, Packer, and Vault. Being the fifth tool in the HashiCorp stack, it focused on providing a way to describe the complete infrastructure as code:

> ... *From physical servers to containers to SaaS products, Terraform is able to create and compose all the components necessary to run any service or application. With Terraform, you describe your complete infrastructure as code, even as it spans multiple service providers. Your servers may come from AWS, your DNS may come from CloudFlare, and your database may come from Heroku. Terraform will build all these resources across all these providers in parallel. Terraform codifies knowledge about your infrastructure unlike any other tool before, and provides the workflow and tooling for safely changing and updating infrastructure.* - https://www.hashicorp.com/blog/terraform.html

Terraform is an open source tool released under Mozilla Public License, version 2.0. The code is stored (as all other tools by HashiCorp) on GitHub, and anyone can contribute to its development.

As a part of its Atlas product, HashiCorp also offers a hosted service named **Terraform Enterprise**, which solves some of the problems that the open source version doesn't handle well. This includes a central facility to run Terraform from access control policies, remote `state` file storage, notifications, built-in GitHub integration, and more. Terraform Enterprise is not covered by this book, but you will learn how to achieve some (if not all) of the same functionalities using only the open source version of Terraform.

Despite the support of over 40 various providers, the main focus of HashiCorp developers is on Amazon Web Services, Google Cloud, and Microsoft Azure. All other providers are developed and supported by the community, meaning that if you are not using the main three, then you might have to contribute to the code base yourself.

> Be really prepared (mentally and skill-wise) to contribute some code yourself, otherwise you might be out of luck. The author of this book faced this issue during a project that relied heavily on OpenStack. It took half a dozen pull requests on GitHub to get OpenStack support for the desired state, and OpenStack is a rather big and popular technology. With lesser-known providers, things can get more complicated very fast, due to a lack of Go libraries for the provider, for example.

Deploying First Server

The code of Terraform is written in the Go programming language, and it is released as a single binary for all major operating systems. Windows, macOS X, FreeBSD, OpenBSD, Salaris, and any Linux distribution are supported in both 32-bit and 64-bit versions.

Terraform is still a relatively new piece of tech, being just a bit over 2 years old. It changes a lot over time and gets new features with every release. The version this book will be using is 0.81.1, and all code samples are guaranteed to run only with this version. That said, Terraform developers are trying to preserve compatibility between minor versions; likely most, if not all, of the code will work with all versions between 0.8.0 and 0.9.0, excluding the latter.

> This book was started when Terraform 0.7 was the latest release. Some companies are still stuck with this version. Because of this, every now and then, you will see tips for 0.7.x releases as well.

Having learned these facts, let's finally proceed to installing Terraform and setting up our workplace.

Preparing work environment

In this book, we will focus on using Terraform in a Linux environment. The general usage of the tool should be the same on all platforms, though some advanced topics and practices discussed in later chapters might apply only to Linux systems.

As mentioned in the previous section, Terraform is distributed as a single binary, packaged inside a ZIP archive. Unfortunately, HashiCorp does not provide native packages for operating systems. That means the first step is to install unzip. Depending on your package manager, this could be done by running `sudo yum install unzip`, or `sudo apt-get install unzip` or it might even already be installed. In any case, after making sure that you can unarchive the ZIP files, proceed to downloading Terraform from the official website, https://www.terraform.io/downloads.html.

Unzip it to any convenient folder. Make sure that this folder is available in your PATH environment variable. A full installation command sequence could look as follows:

```
$> curl -O https://releases.hashicorp.com/terraform/0.8.2/terraform_0.8.2_linux_amd64.zip
$> sudo unzip terraform_0.8.2_linux_amd64.zip -d /usr/local/bin/
```

Deploying First Server

That will extract Terraform binary to `/usr/local/bin`, which is already available in `PATH` on Linux systems.

Finally, let's verify our installation:

```
$> terraform -v
Terraform v0.8.2
```

We have a working Terraform installation now. We are ready to write our first template. First, create an empty directory, name it `packt-terraform`, and enter it:

```
$> mkdir packt-terraform && cd packt-terraform
```

When you run Terraform commands, they look for files with the `.tf` extension in the directory you run them from. They don't take files from subdirectories. *Be careful:* Terraform will load all files with the `.tf` extension if you run it without arguments.

Let's create our very first, not yet very useful, template:

```
$> touch template.tf
```

To apply the template, you need to run the `terraform apply` command. What does this *applying* mean? In Terraform, when you run `apply`, it will read your templates and it will try to create an infrastructure exactly as it's defined in your templates. We will go deeper into how Terraform exactly processes templates in a later chapter.

For now, let's just apply our empty template:

```
$> terraform apply
Apply complete! Resources: 0 added, 0 changed, 0 destroyed.
```

After each run is finished, you get the number of resources that you've added, changed, and destroyed. In this case, it did nothing, as we just have an empty file instead of a real template.

To make Terraform do something useful, we first need to configure our provider, and even before that, we need to find out what a provider is.

The many Terraform providers

Providers are something you use to configure access to the service you create resources for. For example, if you want to create AWS resources, you need to configure the AWS provider. This would specify credentials to access the APIs of many AWS services.

At the time of writing, Terraform has more than 40 providers. This impressive list includes not only major cloud providers such as AWS and Google Cloud, but also smaller services, such as Fastly, a **Content Delivery Network (CDN)** provider.

Not every provider requires explicit configuration. Some of them do not even deal with external services. Instead, they provide resources for local entities. For example, you could use a TLS provider to generate keys and certificates.

Nevertheless, most providers deal with one or another external API and require configuration. In this book, we will be using the AWS provider. Before we configure it, let's have a short introduction to AWS. If you are already familiar with this platform, feel free to skip the next section and proceed directly to *Configuring AWS provider*.

Short introduction to AWS

Amazon Web Services is a cloud offering from Amazon, an online retail giant. Back in the early 2000s, Amazon invested money in an automated platform, which would provide services for things such as network, storage, and computation to Amazon developers. Developers then didn't need to manage underlying the infrastructure. Instead, they would use provided services via APIs to provision virtual machines, storage buckets, and so on.

The platform, initially built to power Amazon itself, was open for public usage in 2006. The first released service was **Simple Queue Service (SQS)**, followed by the two most commonly used AWS services--**Simple Storage Service (S3)** and **Elastic Compute Cloud (EC2)** were released and anyone could pay to use them.

Fast forward 10 years. AWS now has over 70 different services, covering practically everything a modern infrastructure would need. It has services for virtual networking, queue processing, transactional emails, storage, DNS, relational databases, and many, many others. Businesses such as Netflix completely moved away from in-house hardware and instead are building new types of infrastructure on top of cloud resources, getting significant benefits in terms of flexibility and cost-savings, and focusing on working on a product, rather than scaling and maturing their own data center. For more information, refer to the following URL:

```
http://www.datacenterknowledge.com/archives/2016/02/11/netflix-shuts-down-
final-bits-of-own-data-center-infrastructure/
```

With such an impressive list of services, it becomes increasingly hard to juggle all the involved components via AWS Management Console: the in-browser interface for working with AWS. Of course, AWS provides APIs for almost every service it has, but once again, the number and intersection of them can be very high, and it only grows as you keep relying on the cloud. This has led exactly to the set of problems discussed in `Chapter 1`, *Infrastructure Automation*, you end up either with intense ClickOps practices, or you script everything you can.

These problems make AWS a perfect candidate to explore Terraform, as we can fully understand the pain caused by direct usage of its services. Of course, AWS is not free to use, but luckily, for a long time now, they have provided **Free Tier**. Free Tier allows you to use lots (but not all) services for free with certain limitations. For example, you can use a single EC2 instance for 750 hours a month, for 12 months, for free, as long as it has the `t2.micro` type.

> EC2 instances are simply virtual servers. You pay for them per-hour of usage, and you can choose from a predefined list of types. Types are just different combinations of characteristics. Some are optimized for high memory usage; others were created for processor-heavy tasks.

Let's create a brand new AWS account for our Terraform learning goals:

1. Open `https://aws.amazon.com/free` and click on **CREATE A FREE ACCOUNT**.
2. Follow the on screen instructions to complete registration.

> Please note that, in order to use Free Tier, you have to provide your credit card details. However, you won't be charged unless you exceed your free usage limit.

Using Elastic Compute Cloud

We will look at three ways of creating an EC2 instance: manually via the Management Console, with the AWS **Command Line Interface** (**CLI**), and with Terraform.

Creating an instance through the Management Console

Just to get a feel of the AWS Management Console and to fully understand how much Terraform simplifies working with AWS, let's create a single EC2 instance manually:

1. Log in to the console and choose **EC2** from the list of services:

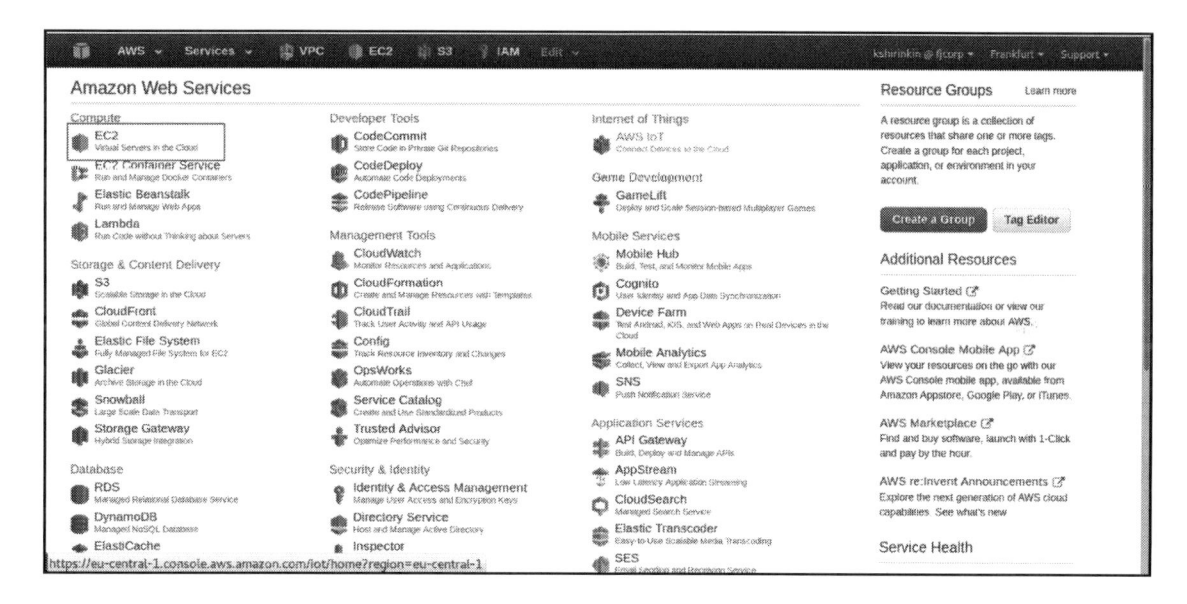

Deploying First Server

2. Click on **Launch Instance**:

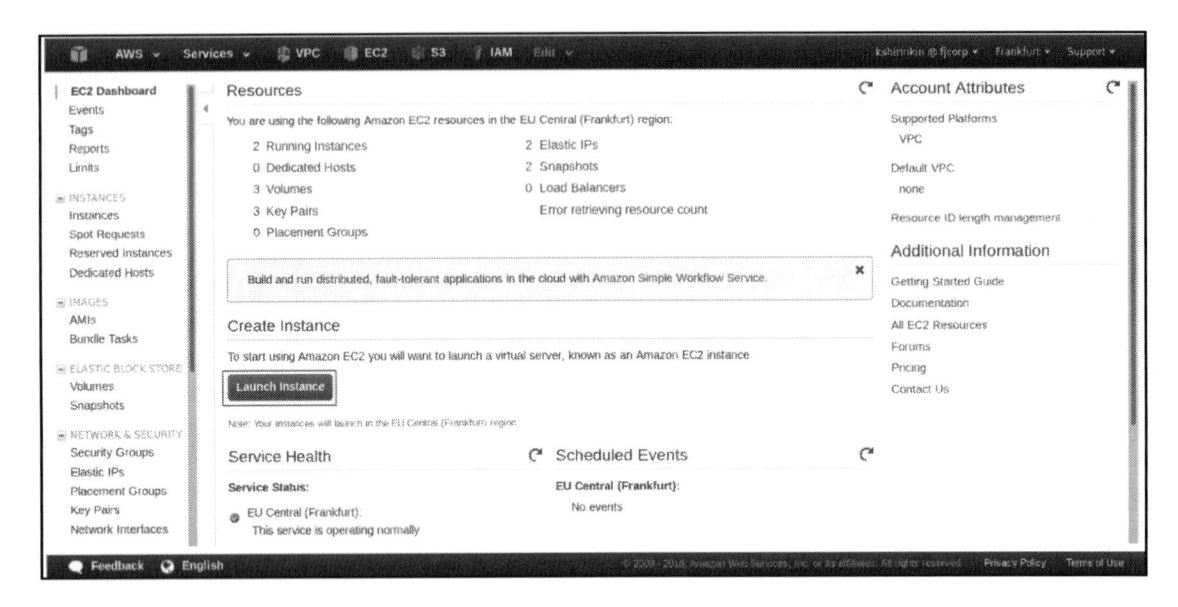

3. Choose **AWS** Marketplace from the left sidebar, type **Centos** in the search box, and click on the **Select** button for the first search result:

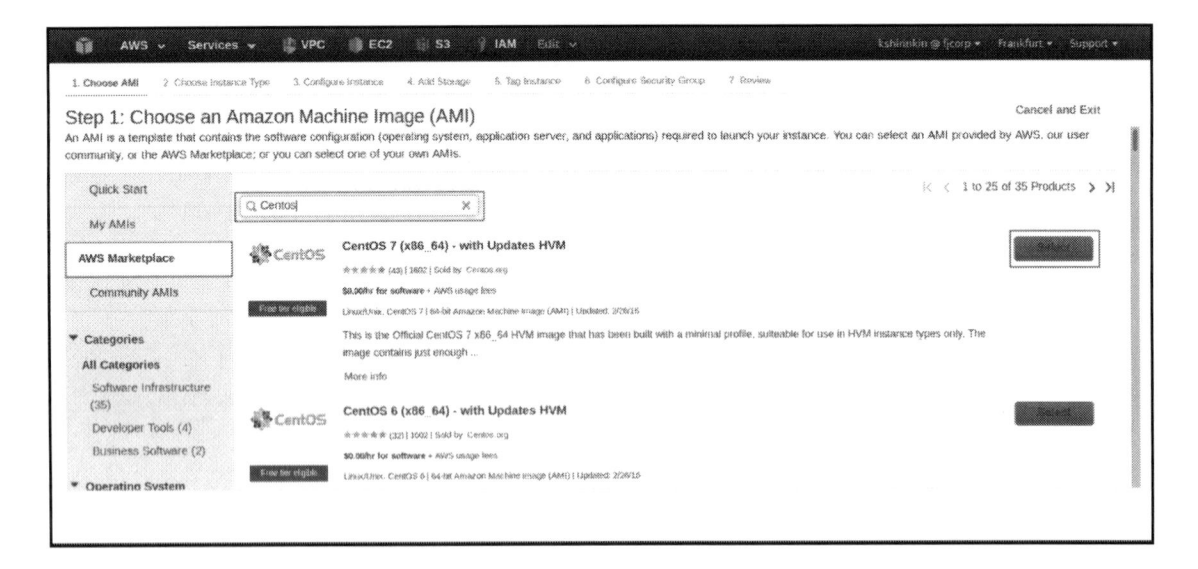

4. On each of the next pages, just click on **Next** till you reach the end of the process and you get a notification as follows:

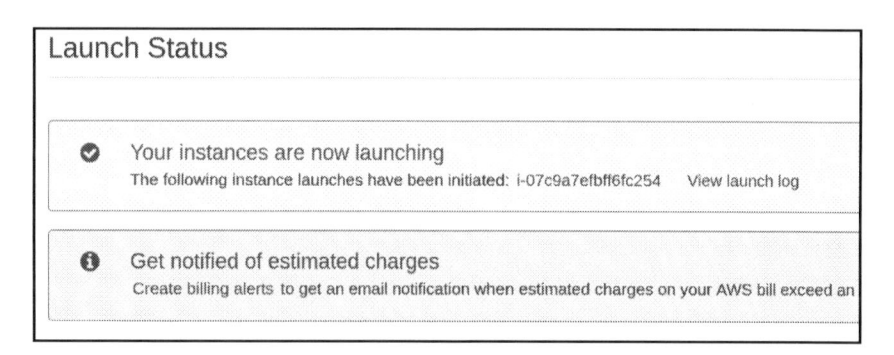

> **Launch Status**
>
> ✓ Your instances are now launching
>   The following instance launches have been initiated: i-07c9a7efbff6fc254   View launch log
>
> ⓘ Get notified of estimated charges
>   Create billing alerts to get an email notification when estimated charges on your AWS bill exceed an

As you see, it's not really a quick process to create a single virtual server on EC2. You have to choose an AMI, an instance type, configure network details and permissions, select or generate an `SSH` key, properly tag it, pick the right security groups, and add storage. Imagine that your day would consist only of manual tasks such as this. What a boring job would it be?

> AMI is a source image an instance is created from. You can create your own AMIs, use the ones provided by AWS, or select one from a community at AWS Marketplace. A **Security Groups** (**SG**) is like a firewall. You can attach multiple SGs to an instance and define inbound and outbound rules. It allows you to configure access not only for IP ranges, but also for other security groups.

And, of course, we looked at only a single service: EC2. As you know already, there are over 70 of them, each with its own interface to click through. Let's take a look now at how to achieve the same with AWS CLI.

Creating an instance with AWS CLI

The AWS provides CLI to interact with its APIs. It's written in Python. You can follow installation instructions from the official guide to get started. Here is the link; `https://aws.amazon.com/cli/`.

Deploying First Server

Perhaps the most important part of setting up AWS CLI is access key configuration. We will also need these keys for Terraform. To get them, click on your username in the top-right part of the AWS Management Console, click on **Security Credentials,** and then download your keys from the **Access Keys (Access Key ID and Secret Access Key)** menu:

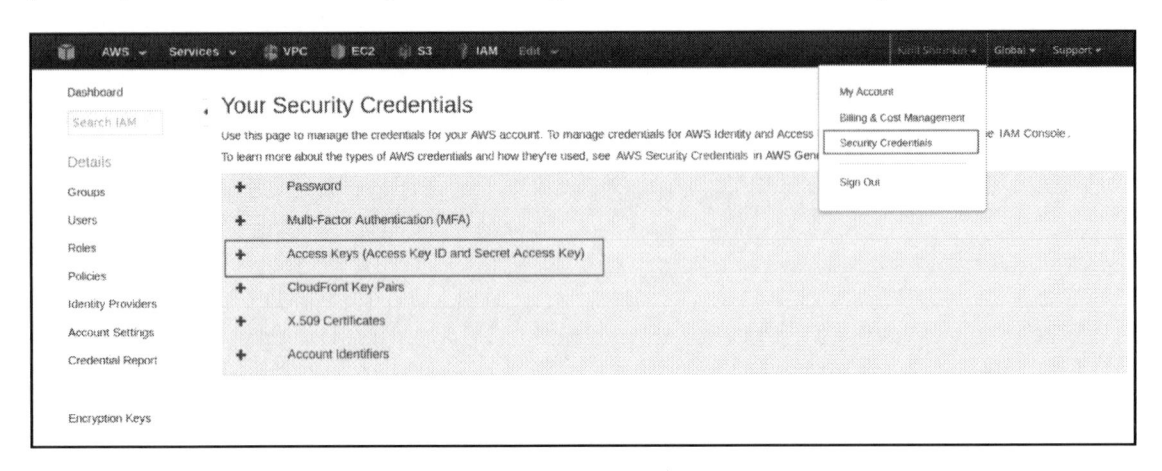

> Using root account access keys is considered a bad practice when working with AWS. You should use IAM users and per-user keys. For the needs of this book, root keys are okay, but as soon as you move production systems to AWS, consider using IAM and reducing root account usage to a minimum. Consider reading and applying AWS **IAM Best Practices** from `http://docs.aws.amazon.com/IAM/latest/UserGuide/best-practices.html`.

Once AWS CLI is installed, run the `aws configure` command. It will prompt you for your access key and region. Once you are finished, you can use it to talk to AWS API. Creating an EC2 instance will look as follows:

```
$> aws ec2 run-instances --image-id ami-xxxxxxxx
                                    --count 1
                                    --instance-type t2.micro
                                    --key-name MyKeyPair
                                    --security-groups my-sg
```

While already much better than doing it from the Management Console, it's still a long command to execute, and it covers only the creation of an instance. To track whether the instance is still there and to update and destroy this instance, you need to construct a similar long sequence of command-line commands. Let's finally do it properly with Terraform.

Configuring AWS provider

Before using Terraform to create an instance, we need to configure AWS provider. This is the first piece of code we will write in our template. Templates are written in a special language named **HashiCorp Configuration Language** (HCL). More details about HCL can be found at https://github.com/hashicorp/hcl. You can also write your templates in JSON, but this is recommended only if a template is itself generated or read by a machine.

We can configure credentials in the following ways.

Static credentials

With this method, you just hardcode your access keys right inside your template. It looks as follows:

```
provider "aws" {
    access_key = "xxxxxxxxxxxx"
    secret_key = "xxxxxxxxxxxx"
    region = "us-east-1"
}
```

Though the simplest one, it is also the least flexible and secure. You don't want to give your credentials just like this to everyone in the team. Rather, each team member should use his or her own keys. Consider this method a bad practice and avoid it when possible.

Environment variables

If not specified in the template, Terraform will try to read configuration from the environment variables `AWS_ACCESS_KEY_ID` and `AWS_SECRET_ACCESS_KEY`. You can also set your region with the `AWS_DEFAULT_REGION` variable. In this case, complete configuration goes down to the following:

```
provider "aws" {}
```

Credentials file

If Terraform can't find keys in the template or environment variables, it will try to fetch them from the credentials file, which is typically stored in the `~/.aws/` credentials. If you have previously installed and configured AWS CLI, then you already have a credentials file generated for you. If you have not done this, then you can add it yourself, with the content as follows:

```
[default]
aws_access_key_id =    xxxxxxxxxxxxx
aws_secret_access_key =   xxxxxxxxxxxxx
```

You should always avoid setting credentials directly in the template. It's up to you whether you use environment variables or a credentials file. Whichever method you picked, let's add the following configuration to `template.tf`:

```
provider "aws" {
  region = "eu-central-1"
}
```

Running the `terraform apply` command still won't do anything because we did not specify any resources we want our infrastructure to have. Let's do that now.

Creating an EC2 instance with Terraform

Resources are components of your infrastructure. They can be something as complex as a complete virtual server, or something as simple as a DNS record. Each resource belongs to a provider, and the type of the resource is suffixed with the provider name. The configuration of a resource takes the following form:

```
resource "provider-name_resource-type" "resource-name" {
  parameter_name = parameter_value
}
```

The combination of resource type and resource name must be unique in your template; otherwise Terraform will complain.

There are three types of things you can configure inside a resource block: resource-specific parameters, meta-parameters, and provisioners. For now, let's focus on resource-specific parameters. They are unique to each resource type.

We will create an EC2 instance. The `aws_instance` resource is responsible for this job. To create an instance, we need to set at least two parameters: `ami` and `instance_type`. Some parameters are required, whereas others are optional, `ami` and `instance_type` being the required ones.

> You can always check the complete list of available parameters in the docs, on the page dedicated to the particular resource. For example, to get the list and description of all the `aws_instance` resource parameters, check out https://www.terraform.io/docs/providers/aws/r/instance.html.

We'll be using the official Centos 7 AMI. As we configured the AWS region to be eu-central-1, we have to use an AMI with the ID `ami-9bf712f4`. We will use the `t2.micro` instance type, as it's the cheapest one and is available as part of the Free Tier offering.

Update the template to look as follows:

```
# Provider configuration
provider "aws" {
  region = "eu-central-1"
}
# Resource configuration
resource "aws_instance" "hello-instance" {
  ami = "ami-9bf712f4"
  instance_type = "t2.micro"
  tags {
    Name = "hello-instance"
  }
}
```

> You might also need to specify the `subnet_id` parameter if you don't have a default VPC. For this, you will need to create a VPC and a subnet. You can either do it now yourself or wait till the next chapter, where we will be extending our template with VPC support. Don't worry if you don't know what VPC is. We will figure it out pretty soon.

As you will have noted, HCL allows commenting your code using a hash sign in front of the text you want to be commented.

Another thing to look at is the `tags` parameter. Terraform is not limited to simple string values. You can also have numbers, Boolean values (`true`, `false`), lists (`["elem1", "elem2", "elem3"]`), and maps. The `tags` parameter is a map of tags for the instance.

Deploying First Server

Let's apply this template!

```
$> terraform apply
aws_instance.hello-instance: Creating...
  ami:                        "" => "ami-378f925b"
  < ....................... >
  instance_type:              "" => "t2.micro"
  key_name:                   "" => "<computed>"
  < ....................... >
  tags.%:                     "" => "1"
  tags.Name:                  "" => "hello-instance"
  tenancy:                    "" => "<computed>"
  vpc_security_group_ids.#:   "" => "<computed>"
aws_instance.hello-instance: Still creating... (10s elapsed)
aws_instance.hello-instance: Still creating... (20s elapsed)
aws_instance.hello-instance: Still creating... (30s elapsed)
aws_instance.hello-instance: Creation complete

Apply complete! Resources: 1 added, 0 changed, 0 destroyed.

The state of your infrastructure has been saved to the path
below. This state is required to modify and destroy your
infrastructure, so keep it safe. To inspect the complete state
use the `terraform show` command.
State path: terraform.tfstate
```

Wow, that's a lot of output for a simple command creating a single instance. Some parts of it were replaced with arrow-wrapped dots, so don't be surprised when you see even more parameter values when you actually run the command. Before digging into the output, let's first verify that the instance was really created in the AWS Management Console:

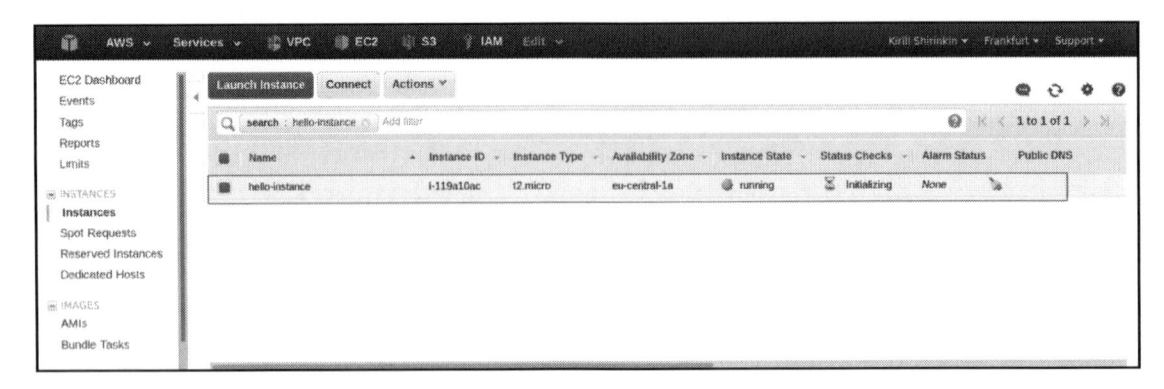

With just 12 lines of code and a single Terraform command invocation, we got our EC2 instance running. So far, the result we got is not that different from using AWS CLI, though: we only created a resource. What is of more interest is how we update and destroy this instance using the same template. To understand how Terraform does it, you need to learn what the `state` file is.

Working with state

If you've read the output of the `terraform apply` command carefully, you might be really curious about what this part means:

```
The state of your infrastructure has been saved to the path
below. This state is required to modify and destroy your
infrastructure, so keep it safe. To inspect the complete state
use the `terraform show` command.
State path: terraform.tfstate
```

What it means is that Terraform didn't simply create an instance and forget about it. It actually saved everything it knows about this instance to a special file, named the `state` file. In this file, Terraform stores the `state` of all the resources it created. This file is saved to the same directory where the Terraform template is, with the `.tfstate` extension. The format of the `state` file is simple `json`. Let's take a look at it piece by piece.

```
{
    "version": 3,
    "terraform_version": "0.8.2",
    "serial": 1,
    "lineage": "65a6dc1b-3f42-4f23-8df1-8b2275602aff",
```

- First of all, Terraform specifies the `version` of the `state` file. It's not the version of this particular state; it's a version of a format of `state` files in general. This allows Terraform to move the format of the `state` file forward without breaking compatibility with older versions.
- The `terraform_version` key is self-explanatory: it's the version of Terraform that the `state` file was created with. If you try to use Terraform 0.7 with a `state` file that specifies version 0.8.2, Terraform will not allow you to do so.

Deploying First Server

- The `serial` key is increased every time you update your `state`, even with the smallest modifications. It is used by Terraform to detect potentially conflicting updates.
- The `lineage` key is set only when you create a new state file. After this, the value of `lineage` is never updated and is not currently used by Terraform. It is planned to be used in order to reduce mistakes when working with remote `state` files, which we will discuss in later chapters.

What goes next in the `state` file are actually resources you've created. Terraform obtains all the information possible about the resources and writes it to the `state` file:

```
"modules": [
    {
        "path": [
            "root"
        ],
        "outputs": {},
        "resources": {
            "aws_instance.hello-instance": {
                "type": "aws_instance",
                "depends_on": [],
                "primary": {
                    "id": "i-06f88fe6a2b4307b8",
                    "attributes": {
                        "ami": "ami-9bf712f4",
                        "availability_zone": "eu-central-1a",
                        "disable_api_termination": "false",
                        "ebs_block_device.#": "0",
                        "ebs_optimized": "false",
                        "ephemeral_block_device.#": "0",
                        "iam_instance_profile": "",
                        "id": "i-06f88fe6a2b4307b8",
```

You've never specified parameters such as availability zone or `disable_api_termination`, and yet Terraform has them in the `state` file.

The `state` file is what makes Terraform capable of not only creating, but also updating and destroying infrastructure. Terraform knows if the actual state of resources has changed and if parameters in a template have changed, and then it intelligently figures out what the final state should look like and gets your infrastructure to that state.

This makes the `state` file so important that you never want to lose it after you have created your environment. Losing the `state` file means losing control of your environment through Terraform. It can be very frustrating to create a huge test environment, delete the `state` file by accident, and then delete all resources manually through the AWS Management Console.

The `state` file was not made to read by humans. But Terraform has multiple commands that allow you to view and modify the `state` file conveniently. The `terraform state list` command will list all resources in the `state` file:

```
$> terraform state list
aws_instance.hello-instance
```

The `terraform show` command will print a complete state in a human-readable format:

```
$> terraform show
aws_instance.hello-instance:
  id = i-06f88fe6a2b4307b8
  ami = ami-9bf712f4
  availability_zone = eu-central-1a
  disable_api_termination = false
  ebs_block_device.# = 0
  ebs_optimized = false
  ephemeral_block_device.# = 0
  iam_instance_profile =
  instance_state = running
  instance_type = t2.micro
  key_name =
  monitoring = false
  ...
```

If you want to view the details of only one resource, you can use `terraform state show path_to_resource`. Running `terraform state show aws_instance.hello-instance` will give you all the details about the created instance.

After talking so much about how useful the `state` file is, let's finally use Terraform to update the instance.

Handling resource updates

Let's change our instance's name to be `hello-updated-instance`:

```
resource "aws_instance" "hello-instance" {
  ami = "ami-9bf712f4"
  instance_type = "t2.micro"
  subnet_id = "subnet-5f22f536"
  tags {
    Name = "hello-update-instance"
  }
}
```

Before we actually run the update, wouldn't it be useful to see what exactly Terraform do when we run the `terraform apply` command again? Luckily, there is the `terraform plan` command that does exactly the same, that is, it shows you what applying do by checking the template, `state` file, and actual state of the resource:

```
$> terraform plan
Refreshing Terraform state in-memory prior to plan...
The refreshed state will be used to calculate this plan, but
will not be persisted to local or remote state storage.
aws_instance.hello-instance: Refreshing state... (ID: i-119a10ac)
The Terraform execution plan has been generated and is shown below.
Resources are shown in alphabetical order for quick scanning. Green resources
will be created (or destroyed and then created if an existing resource
exists), yellow resources are being changed in-place, and red resources
will be destroyed. Cyan entries are data sources to be read.
Note: You didn't specify an "-out" parameter to save this plan, so when
"apply" is called, Terraform can't guarantee this is what will execute.
~ aws_instance.hello-instance
    tags.Name: "hello-instance" => "hello-update-instance"
Plan: 0 to add, 1 to change, 0 to destroy.
```

It's a good practice to always run plan before apply. This saves you from accidental deletion or resource updates that you didn't plan to have.

We can also check whether the template file is valid with the `terraform validate` command. Remove one of (any of) the equal signs from your template, then run this command to get a result similar to the following:

```
$> terraform validate
Error loading files Error parsing /home/kshirinkin/work/packt-terraform-
rewrites
/template.tf: At 9:17: nested object expected: LBRACE got: ASSIGN
```

Another nice command is `terraform fmt`. Similar to (and likely inspired by) the Go `go fmt` command, `terraform fmt` will format your template file to comply with best practices. If you run it, then your code will be aligned a bit more nicely:

```
# Resource configuration
resource "aws_instance" "hello-instance" {
  ami           = "ami-9bf712f4"
  instance_type = "t2.micro"
  subnet_id     = "subnet-5f22f536"

  tags {
    Name = "hello-update-instance"
  }
}
```

It looks like nothing terrible will happen if we run the `terraform apply` command, so let's go ahead and do it:

```
$> terraform apply
aws_instance.hello-instance: Refreshing state... (ID:
i-06f88fe6a2b4307b8)
aws_instance.hello-instance: Modifying...
  tags.Name: "hello-instance" => "hello-update-instance"
aws_instance.hello-instance: Modifications complete
Apply complete! Resources: 0 added, 1 changed, 0 destroyed.
The state of your infrastructure has been saved to the path
below. This state is required to modify and destroy your
infrastructure, so keep it safe. To inspect the complete state
use the `terraform show` command.
State path: terraform.tfstate
```

Deploying First Server

Terraform successfully modified our instance. Let's see what happened to our `state` file:

```
$> head terraform.tfstate
{
    "version": 3,
    "terraform_version": "0.8.2",
    "serial": 1,
    "lineage": "65a6dc1b-3f42-4f23-8df1-8b2275602aff",
    "modules": [
        {
            "path": [
                "root"
            ],
```

As expected, Terraform increased the `serial` key, as it does for every Terraform run. We are not going to need this specific instance any more. We can safely destroy it now.

Destroying everything we've built

Destroying infrastructure with Terraform is as, easy as or even easier than, creating it. All you need to do is to run the `terraform destroy` command, as shown here:

```
$> terraform destroy
Do you really want to destroy?
  Terraform will delete all your managed infrastructure.
  There is no undo. Only 'yes' will be accepted to confirm.
  Enter a value:
```

Terraform is nice enough to ask you for a confirmation, in case you typed the `terraform destroy` command by accident:

```
aws_instance.hello-instance: Refreshing state... (ID: i-06f88fe6a2b4307b8)
aws_instance.hello-instance: Destroying...
aws_instance.hello-instance: Still destroying... (10s elapsed)
aws_instance.hello-instance: Still destroying... (20s elapsed)
aws_instance.hello-instance: Destruction complete
Apply complete! Resources: 0 added, 0 changed, 1 destroyed.
```

If we want to get rid of only one particular resource from our template, we don't need to run the `terraform destroy` command. We could simply remove this resource from `template.tf`, and the next `terraform apply` command will figure out that you don't need this resource any more and destroy it. Try it yourself, by first running the `terraform apply` command to create the instance again, then removing the instance from `template.tf`, and then plan and apply again. In the next chapter, we won't need this particular instance any longer.

Summary

You learned so much in this chapter! After learning some background history about Terraform origins, we wrote our very first template. Then, we took a quick tour of AWS, just to make sure that we are able to use it. After gaining access to EC2, we created an instance in three different ways:

- Via AWS Management Console
- Via AWS CLI
- With Terraform

Using Terraform, baked by its powerful `state` file, gives us a lot of benefits, such as smart update management. By now, we can already create, update, and destroy simple infrastructures with Terraform. However, there is yet so much to learn. How do you specify dependencies between resources? How do you keep the ever-growing size of the template under control? These are the questions we will get answers to in the next chapter.

3
Resource Dependencies and Modules

Previously, we have managed only one resource with Terraform--a single EC2 instance. Obviously, the real infrastructure is much more complicated than a single server. The more resources you have, the more dependencies between them you have to handle. Also, when the number of resources grows, you will have a hard time managing them via a single huge template file.

In this chapter, we will learn about one of the most important features of Terraform: **dependency graph**. We will figure out how dependencies work and see it in practice by creating a complete virtual network via AWS VPC. Then, we will learn how to work around some limitations in dependency handling using some of the advanced Terraform features. Finally, when we find out that our template is too big, we will use Terraform modules to **Don't Repeat Yourself** (**DRY**) our code.

> DRY is a software development principle. Its goal is to reduce the amount of duplication in your code, thus reducing the chances of mistakes and increasing the maintainability of the code.

Creating an AWS Virtual Private Cloud

Perhaps one of the best features of AWS is **Virtual Private Cloud (VPC)**.

In essence, VPC is a virtual network that you can divide into subnets. Some subnets can be public (with access to the internet), and some are private. You can define routing between subnets, and by default, they can freely access each other. You can also create VPN to your VPC, add NAT gateways, manage DHCP options, and define ACLs for your networks. VPC is a complex service with many subtools and options. For our purpose, we will use only a subset of them though.

> **Typical use case for VPC**: Keeping publicly accessible web servers in public subnets and database servers in private ones, and enabling a secure connection between cloud resources and on-premise machines.

Security groups are also a part of AWS VPC. With security groups, you can define inbound and outbound firewall rules and then you can attach these groups to EC2 instances. As a source of traffic for these rules, you can either use IP ranges, IDs of other security groups, or even IDs of other instances.

If you created a new AWS account in the previous chapter, you should have a default VPC. If you have a very old AWS account, then you might not have it. In any case, we won't use any precreated VPCs. Instead, let's start with creating a VPC by making our `template.tf` look as follows:

```
provider "aws" {
  region = "eu-central-1"
}
resource "aws_vpc" "my_vpc" {
  cidr_block = "10.0.0.0/16"
}
```

For each VPC, you need to specify a CIDR block range of IP addresses used for EC2 instances in this VPC. Go ahead and apply the following template:

```
$> terraform apply

aws_vpc.my_vpc: Creating...
  cidr_block:                 "" => "10.0.0.0/16"
  default_network_acl_id:     "" => "<computed>"
  default_security_group_id:  "" => "<computed>"
  dhcp_options_id:            "" => "<computed>"
  enable_classiclink:         "" => "<computed>"
```

Resource Dependencies and Modules

```
    enable_dns_hostnames:       "" => "<computed>"
    enable_dns_support:         "" => "<computed>"
    instance_tenancy:           "" => "<computed>"
    main_route_table_id:        "" => "<computed>"
aws_vpc.my_vpc: Creation complete
Apply complete! Resources: 1 added, 0 changed, 0 destroyed.
```

> In case you are asking yourself what `<computed>` means, it means that the value won't be known until the resource is created.

Creating a VPC is not enough: to be able to place instances in this network, we also need a subnet. This subnet belongs to a previously created VPC. This means that we have to pass a VPC ID when we create it. We don't have to hardcode it though. Terraform, via interpolation syntax, allows us to reference any other resource it manages using the following syntax: `${RESOURCE_TYPE.RESOURCE_NAME.ATTRIBUTE_NAME}`.

Interpolation allows you to reference other resources and variables and call various functions. In the case of resource reference, it saves you from hardcoding their IDs. Terraform will put the required value (in this case, VPC ID) as soon as it has it.

Add the following to the template:

```
resource "aws_subnet" "public" {
    vpc_id = "${aws_vpc.my_vpc.id}"
    cidr_block = "10.0.1.0/24"
}
```

Note the interpolated string: `${aws_vpc.my_vpc.id}`. We referenced the previously created VPC inside a subnet configuration. That's how an interpolation syntax in Terraform looks: you wrap the code with `${}`.

We will take a deeper look at variables and functions a bit later. For now, let's focus on how Terraform handles referencing resources inside other resources. After all, it's backed by one of the most powerful core Terraform features: dependency graph.

Understanding dependency graph

Terraform doesn't simply build your resources and write their configuration into a `state` file. Internally, it also manages a dependency graph of all the resources you have. It's hard to see with a single resource, but now we have two interconnected resources: VPC and a subnet. The latter one depends on the existence of the first one. But wait, what is a dependency graph anyway?

First of all, let's recall what a graph is. We won't go deep into mathematical formulas and advanced graph theories and examples here. Graph theory is big, and there are so many applications of it.

Though there are many definitions of a graph, which differ depending on the knowledge area and industry, the simplest description is *a set of nodes and edges, where edges represent a connection between two nodes*. It's easier to look at a graph than to read about one:

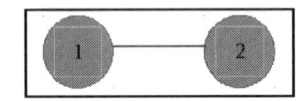

Here, we have two nodes connected to each other. Nothing really complicated. What is a dependency graph then? Let's steal a definition from Wikipedia (`https://en.wikipedia.org/wiki/Dependency_graph`):

> *In mathematics, computer science and digital electronics, a dependency graph is a directed graph representing dependencies of several objects towards each other. It is possible to derive an evaluation order or the absence of an evaluation order that respects the given dependencies from the dependency graph.*

Here, **directed graph** means a graph in which edges have a direction. If we update the preceding graph to be directed, it would look as follows:

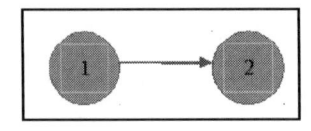

A dependency graph allows us, for example, to properly order the creation or destruction of nodes or to order a set of commands. It's all about ordering, actually. When you use a package manager in your operating system, most likely, some kind of graph is used to resolve dependencies between packages and install the missing ones.

Dependency graphs are used in many places: compilers, package managers, to build scripts such as Make. Also, of course, they are used by Terraform to handle dependencies and the order of creation and deletion of resources.

There are just three types of nodes in a Terraform graph:

- Resource node
- Provider configuration node
- Resource meta-node

What the resource node and provider configuration node are responsible for is clear: the provider node configures a provider (AWS, in our examples) and the resource node manages an entity of this provider (EC2, VPC, and so on, in the case of AWS). A resource meta-node doesn't really do anything special; it is used for convenience and makes a graph more pretty. It is applicable only if you specify a **count** parameter greater than one.

> We will get back to count parameters in Chapter 6, *Scaling and Updating Infrastructure*.

When Terraform builds a graph, it includes resources both in the state file and in your template. It marks the ones that are missing inside the template for destruction. For some resources, it creates multiple nodes. In the case of recreation, there is one node for the destroy action and one for creation, both for the same resource.

Conveniently, there is the `terraform graph` command, which will show you the graph for your template:

```
$> terraform graph
digraph {
    compound = "true"
    newrank = "true"
    subgraph "root" {
            "[root] aws_subnet.public" [label = "aws_subnet.public", shape = "box"]
            "[root] aws_vpc.my_vpc" [label = "aws_vpc.my_vpc", shape = "box"]
            "[root] provider.aws" [label = "provider.aws", shape = "diamond"]
            "[root] aws_subnet.public" -> "[root] aws_vpc.my_vpc"
            "[root] aws_vpc.my_vpc" -> "[root] provider.aws"
    }
}
```

Resource Dependencies and Modules

The output of this command may not look very representative, but it is actually in DOT format, which you can easily convert to a picture. For example, if you have the `GraphViz` package installed, you could do it with the `terraform graph | dot -Tpng > graph.png` command. All further graphs are generated exactly by this command.

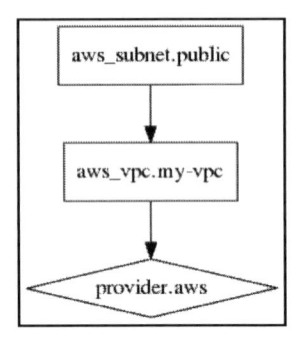

```
aws_subnet.public
       |
       v
aws_vpc.my-vpc
       |
       v
   provider.aws
```

> You can find `GraphViz` packages for various operating systems on the official website `http://www.graphviz.org/`.

Provider nodes are drawn as rhombuses and resources as rectangles. You can clearly see how resources depend on each other in this picture. It is much easier to understand, compared with just looking at the template. We will use graph outputs a lot in this chapter.

Playing with Terraform graphs

Let's play around with our VPC a bit to better understand how resource dependencies are handled. Instead of adding a subnet, let's destroy the complete infrastructure we have so far and then plan creation from scratch:

```
$> terraform destroy
$> terraform plan
    # ...
+ aws_subnet.public
    availability_zone:          "<computed>"
    cidr_block:                 "10.0.1.0/24"      map_public_ip_on_launch: "false"
    vpc_id:                     "${aws_vpc.my_vpc.id}"
    # ...
```

[46]

Resource Dependencies and Modules

Terraform doesn't know the VPC ID yet, so it doesn't show it to you in the plan. Let's apply the template and observe the order of resource creation:

```
$> terraform apply
aws_vpc.my_vpc: Creating...
    cidr_block:                  ""  =>  "10.0.0.0/16"
    default_network_acl_id:      ""  =>  "<computed>"
    default_security_group_id:   ""  =>  "<computed>"
    dhcp_options_id:             ""  =>  "<computed>"
    enable_classiclink:          ""  =>  "<computed>"
    enable_dns_hostnames:        ""  =>  "<computed>"
    enable_dns_support:          ""  =>  "<computed>"
    instance_tenancy:            ""  =>  "<computed>"
    main_route_table_id:         ""  =>  "<computed>"
aws_vpc.my_vpc: Creation complete
aws_subnet.public: Creating...
    availability_zone:           ""  =>  "<computed>"
    cidr_block:                  ""  =>  "10.0.1.0/24"
    map_public_ip_on_launch:     ""  =>  "false"
    vpc_id:                      ""  =>  "vpc-8f8568e7"
aws_subnet.public: Creation complete
```

Terraform knew (from the graph it built) that subnet requires VPC to exist, so it created it first, followed by subnet.

What happens if we recreate the VPC? Let's try it out with the help of the `taint` command. `terraform taint` marks a single resource for recreation. The resource will be destroyed and then created again.

```
$> terraform taint aws_vpc.my_vpc
    The resource aws_vpc.my_vpc in the module root has been marked as
tainted!
$> terraform plan
  -/+ aws_subnet.public
      availability_zone:         "eu-central-1b" => "<computed>"
      cidr_block:                "10.0.1.0/24" => "10.0.1.0/24"
      map_public_ip_on_launch:   "false" => "false"
      vpc_id:                    "vpc-8f8568e7" => "${aws_vpc.my_vpc.id}"
(forces new resource)
  -/+ aws_vpc.my_vpc (tainted)
      cidr_block:                "10.0.0.0/16" => "10.0.0.0/16"
      default_network_acl_id:    "acl-a52febcd" => "<computed>"
      default_security_group_id: "sg-feafde96" => "<computed>"
      dhcp_options_id:           "dopt-b82bc8d1" => "<computed>"
      enable_classiclink:        "" => "<computed>"
      enable_dns_hostnames:      "false" => "<computed>"
      enable_dns_support:        "true" => "<computed>"
```

Resource Dependencies and Modules

```
instance_tenancy:          "default"    => "<computed>"
main_route_table_id:       "rtb-1913d071" => "<computed>"
```

> You might have noted already: in Terraform outputs, – means resource will be destroyed, –/+ means recreation, and + is for creation.

Terraform has got us covered: after recreating a VPC, it will also recreate a subnet because it knows that a subnet depends on the VPC to exist. As AWS doesn't allow simply changing the VPC ID of an existing subnet, Terraform will force the creation of a completely new subnet.

Which parameters the resource will use depends on provider implementation. Normally, it is mentioned in the Terraform documentation page for a specific resource.

If you try to draw a graph again, you won't see much difference from the previous one. The special destroy nodes are not included by default, and in order to see them, you need to specify the -verbose argument:

```
$> terraform graph -verbose | dot -Tpng > graph.png
```

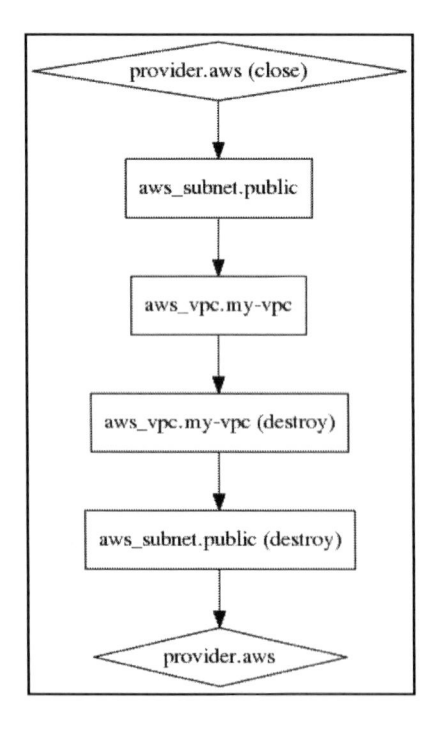

```
provider.aws (close)
        ↓
aws_subnet.public
        ↓
aws_vpc.my-vpc
        ↓
aws_vpc.my-vpc (destroy)
        ↓
aws_subnet.public (destroy)
        ↓
provider.aws
```

> As of Terraform version 0.8.2, the `-verbose` flag seems to be either broken or temporarily disabled and doesn't actually draw destroy nodes. The source code for this flag is still there, deep inside Terraform. The preceding diagram was generated with Terraform 0.7.2.

Now we can see one node of the graph for the existing resource and another node to destroy it. Nodes are added to the graph in an order that will lead to the correct removal of resources that need to be removed.

Before we finish with graphs, let's take a quick look at how dependencies are specified inside the state file:

```
"aws_subnet.public": {
    "type": "aws_subnet",
    "depends_on": [
        "aws_vpc.my_vpc"
      ],
  "primary": {
  "id": "subnet-2116e25b",
  "attributes": {
        "availability_zone": "eu-central-1b",
        "cidr_block": "10.0.1.0/24",
        "id": "subnet-2116e25b",
        "map_public_ip_on_launch": "false",
        "tags.%": "0",
        "vpc_id": "vpc-8f8568e7"
    },
    "meta": {},
    "tainted": false
},
```

Note the `depends_on` part - Terraform saves references to resources, and this one depends on inside this key. Most of the time, dependencies in Terraform just work. You just need to reference resources inside the template and Terraform will do the job of building a graph and order operations with it. But, sometimes, you need a little bit more control over dependencies.

> There is another advantage of graphs inside Terraform - they allow you to process nodes in parallel if they don't depend on each other. By default, up to 10 graph nodes can be processed in parallel. You could specify the -`parallelism` flag for `apply`, `plan`, and `destroy` commands, but it's rather an advanced operation, and in most cases, you don't need it.

Controlling dependencies with depends_on and ignore_changes

In 99% of cases, Terraform will resolve dependencies automatically. There are two problems you can encounter when you rely solely on automatic resolution:

- Dependency is not automatically handled by Terraform
- Dependency leads to unwanted behavior and should be omitted

For both problems, there is a solution in Terraform. Let's first look at how you can force dependencies with `depends_on`. For each resource, you can specify the `depends_on` parameter, which accepts a list of resources that this resource depends on. As a result, this resource won't be created until the ones listed inside this parameter are created.

There might be different use cases for this. For example, your private OpenStack installation could be implemented in a way such that it is impossible to create virtual routers in parallel, so you have to force dependency for each router to force Terraform to create them one after another. Or your instances could depend on the existence of one central master instance (which could be Chef server or Puppet master). Let's implement this scenario in our template.

Add two new resources to `template.tf`:

```
resource "aws_instance" "master-instance" {
  ami = "ami-9bf712f4"
  instance_type = "t2.micro"
  subnet_id = "${aws_subnet.public.id}"
}
resource "aws_instance" "slave-instance" {
  ami = "ami-9bf712f4"
  instance_type = "t2.micro"
  subnet_id = "${aws_subnet.public.id}"
  depends_on = ["aws_instance.master-instance"]
}
```

Draw the `graph`:

```
$> terraform graph | dot -Tpng > graph.png
```

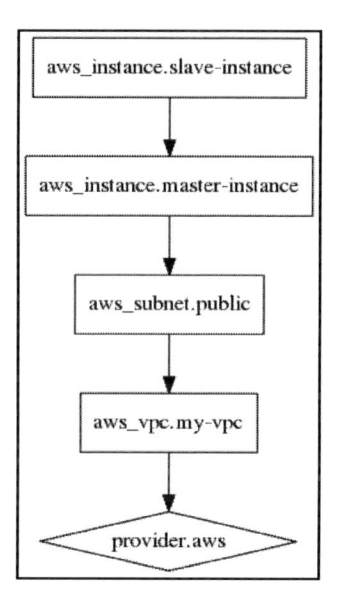

```
aws_instance.slave-instance
          │
          ▼
aws_instance.master-instance
          │
          ▼
   aws_subnet.public
          │
          ▼
    aws_vpc.my-vpc
          │
          ▼
     provider.aws
```

Let's remove `depends_on` for the slave instance and draw `graph` again:

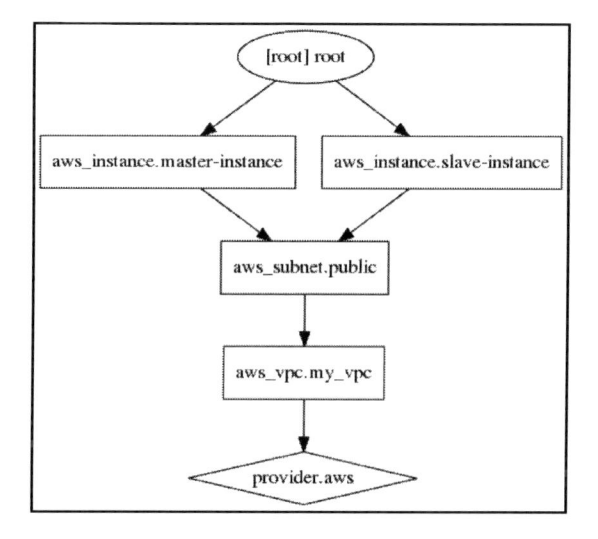

```
              [root] root
              /         \
             ▼           ▼
aws_instance.master-instance   aws_instance.slave-instance
             \           /
              ▼         ▼
          aws_subnet.public
                  │
                  ▼
           aws_vpc.my_vpc
                  │
                  ▼
            provider.aws
```

Resource Dependencies and Modules

With `depends_on`, all resources would be created sequentially. Without it, both EC2 instances will be created in parallel.

> Don't be too confused about the **root** circle. We will talk about what it is in a couple of minutes.

Now, let's say we want to include a private `hostname` of `master` in the list of `tags` of the slave, but we don't want to update it if `master` was recreated. To achieve this, we will use the `ignore_changes` parameter. This parameter is part of `lifecycle` block, responsible for a few other create/destroy-related parameters. The `ignore_changes` parameter accepts the list of parameters to ignore when updating, in our case -`tags`:

```
resource "aws_instance" "slave-instance" {
  ami = "ami-9bf712f4"
  instance_type = "t2.micro"
  subnet_id = "${aws_subnet.public.id}"
  tags {
    master_hostname = "${aws_instance.master-instance.private_dns}"
  }
  lifecycle {
    ignore_changes = ["tags"]
  }
}
```

Run the `terraform apply` command, then remove the `tags` parameter from the `aws_instance.slave` instance configuration and run the `terraform plan` command. Terraform will show you that there is nothing to do because it was told to ignore changes of the `tags` parameter.

> The most common use case for `ignore_changes` is, perhaps, `user_data` for cloud instances. For most providers, if you change `user_data` (the script to be executed on instance creation by the `cloud-init` utility), Terraform will try to recreate the instance. It is often unwanted behavior because, most likely, you use the same `user_data` string for multiple instances and you want changes to be applied only for new instances, while keeping the others running (or by recreating them one by one yourself).

[52]

With `depends_on` and `ignore_changes`, you can achieve a bit more flexibility when dealing with dependencies inside Terraform.

There are two other life cycle block parameters that should be mentioned:

- The `create_before_destroy` Boolean parameter allows us to tell Terraform to first create a new resource and then destroy the previous one in the case of recreation.
- The `prevent_destroy` parameter, also Boolean, marks a resource as indestructible and can save you some nerves. One example of a resource that can benefit from this option is an Elastic IP - a dedicated IP address inside AWS that you can attach to an EC2 instance.

Making sense of our template

So far, we have created a VPC with a single subnet. While we played around with master-slave instances and dependencies between them, these were just temporal changes to show how Terraform handles these use cases. Now it's time to add more meat to the template: let's create an instance with a security group attached to it.

Let's say we have a web application named *MightyTrousers* and we need a server for this, protected from unwanted traffic by a security group:

```
resource "aws_security_group" "allow_http" {
  name = "allow_http"
  description = "Allow HTTP traffic"
  vpc_id = "${aws_vpc.my_vpc.id}"

  ingress {
    from_port = 80
    to_port = 80
    protocol = "tcp"
    cidr_blocks = ["0.0.0.0/0"]
  }

  egress {
    from_port = 0
    to_port = 0
    protocol = "-1"
    cidr_blocks = ["0.0.0.0/0"]
  }
}
```

```
resource "aws_instance" "mighty-trousers" {
  ami = "ami-9bf712f4"
  instance_type = "t2.micro"
  subnet_id = "${aws_subnet.public.id}"
  vpc_security_group_ids = ["${aws_security_group.allow_http.id}"]
}
```

Given that we have only a single web application, our Terraform template would represent a complete production-ready template for the whole infrastructure. It handles dependencies very well, updates changes, and in general, solves the problem of templating all used AWS services. The problem is that a single VPC with a single server is probably the least complicated infrastructure one could imagine. But it's a good start.

After a little while, your company grows beyond the original small web application, of course. Developers have written a new app, named *CrazyFoods*. Now you need to template it too.

At first, we will be tempted to simply copy and paste the configuration of the *MightyTrousers* application, replace some strings in a few places, and call it a day. But soon we realize that that wouldn't be a job well done: we would have just duplicated a bunch of code for no reason. As we really want both applications to have the same setup, we now have to make sure that this huge new template is properly updated in two places--once for the *MightyTrousers* application (security group + instance) and then again for the *CrazyFoods* app (also a security group + instance).

Wouldn't it be nice to reuse the existing configuration and update it from a single place? Enter Terraform modules.

Removing duplication with modules

Modules in Terraform are used to group multiple resources. You can reuse this grouping multiple times. You can also configure modules with variables, and modules can return output that you can pass to other resources and modules.

To get started with modules, create a folder named `modules` in the same folder as the `template.tf`. Inside this folder, create another one, named `application`. In this folder, we will keep the module responsible for creating all the resources required by a single application, be it *MightyTrousers*, *CrazyFoods*, or anything else.

Resource Dependencies and Modules

A module is a regular Terraform template, so just create the
`./modules/application/application.tf` file with the following contents:

```
resource "aws_security_group" "allow_http" {
  name = "allow_http"
  description = "Allow HTTP traffic"
  vpc_id = "${aws_vpc.my_vpc.id}"
  ingress {
    from_port = 80
    to_port = 80
    protocol = "tcp"
    cidr_blocks = ["0.0.0.0/0"]
  }

  egress {
    from_port = 0
    to_port = 0
    protocol = "-1"
    cidr_blocks = ["0.0.0.0/0"]
  }
}
resource "aws_instance" "mighty-trousers" {
  ami = "ami-9bf712f4"
  instance_type = "t2.micro"
  subnet_id = "${aws_subnet.public.id}"
  vpc_security_group_ids = ["${aws_security_group.allow_http.id}"]
}
```

Now, with this module in place, let's actually call it inside our `template.tf`. Remove everything related to the *MightyTrousers* application and add the following `module` configuration:

```
module "mighty_trousers" {
  source = "./modules/application"
}
```

The name of the module (`mighty_trousers`) is only used to reference this module in other places in the template. We can name modules any way we like, as long as they are unique.

Now, let's try to apply this template as usual: `terraform apply`:

```
Error downloading modules: module mighty_trousers: not found, may need to be
downloaded using 'terraform get'
```

[55]

Resource Dependencies and Modules

Even though we specified a source, Terraform still can't find our module. It requires you to run the `terraform get` command first.

When you run this command, Terraform downloads the module to the `.terraform` folder inside your project's folder. If your module is local to your laptop, Terraform will simply create a **symlink** from it to the `.terraform` folder.

There are other types of sources for modules. You could specify a Git repository, HTTP URL, GitHub, and BitBucket links as a module source. In large organizations, there are probably many different Terraform modules, and it's convenient to store them outside of project-specific repository. Every time you run the `get` command, it will pull it from the source and save it inside the `.terraform` folder.

> Segment.com, an analytics and data platform company, open sources their Terraform modules: https://github.com/segmentio/stack. As they claim, it's a set of Terraform modules to configure production infrastructure with AWS. There is also a `terraform-comunity-modules` GitHub organization, https://github.com/terraform-community-modules, which has many different modules you could reuse or be inspired by. In future, as Terraform adoption among companies grows, we might see many more open source, third-party reusable, ready for production modules, just as we use Puppet modules or Chef cookbooks today.

If you run the `terraform get` command, you will get the following output with errors:

```
$> terraform get
Get: file:///home/kshirinkin/work/packt-terraform-rewrites/modules/application
Error loading Terraform: module mighty_trousers.root: 2 error(s) occurred:
    * resource 'aws_security_group.allow_http' config: unknown resource 'aws_vpc.my_vpc' referenced in variable aws_vpc.my_vpc.id
    * resource 'aws_instance.mighty-trousers' config: unknown resource 'aws_subnet.public' referenced in variable aws_subnet.public.id
```

This is nothing to be surprised about: we blindly copied and pasted our *MightyTrousers* application configuration. This configuration references resources defined in the main `template.tf`. But these resources are not available inside the module template! We need a way to pass required values down to the module. Module variables are exactly what we need.

Configuring modules

Let's list the data we need to pass to the module:

- Name of the application
- VPC ID
- Subnet ID

That should be sufficient for now. Update the module inside `template.tf` to look as follows:

```
module "mighty_trousers" {
  source = "./modules/application"
  vpc_id = "${aws_vpc.my_vpc.id}"
  subnet_id = "${aws_subnet.public.id}"
  name = "MightyTrousers"
}
```

Passing data like this is not enough though. We need to define variables inside the module template. The thing is, our `tempate.tf` is a module itself, a special module named **root module**. That's what you saw on the last graph we drew--resources were coming from the root module. So, we were actually already using modules all this time, and every module, including the root module, can be configured with variables.

> We have not looked much into Terraform variables in general till now, and most of the content on this topic is explained in `Chapter 4`, *Storing and Supplying Configuration*. For now, let's get a short introduction to them.

Variables are defined with the `variable` keyboard, followed by the variable name and optional default value inside curly braces:

```
variable number_of_servers { default = 1 }
```

There are many ways to define variables, and there are multiple types of variables, but let's save our in-depth exploration for the next chapter. For now, let's add the following lines to the top of the `./modules/application/application.tf` file:

```
variable "vpc_id"    {}
variable "subnet_id" {}
variable "name"      {}
```

Resource Dependencies and Modules

To use the variable, you need to reference it via a special `var` keyword, as follows: `${var.my_variable}`. Replace all the resource references with variables:

```
resource "aws_security_group" "allow_http" {
  name = "${var.name} allow_http"
  description = "Allow HTTP traffic"
  vpc_id = "${var.vpc_id}"

  ingress {
    from_port = 80
    to_port = 80
    protocol = "tcp"
    cidr_blocks = ["0.0.0.0/0"]
  }
  egress {
    from_port = 0
    to_port = 0
    protocol = "-1"
    cidr_blocks = ["0.0.0.0/0"]
  }
}
resource "aws_instance" "app-server" {
  ami = "ami-9bf712f4"
  instance_type = "t2.micro"
  subnet_id = "${var.subnet_id}"
  vpc_security_group_ids = ["${aws_security_group.allow_http.id}"]
  tags {
    Name = "${var.name}"
  }
}
```

Now you should be able to run again via the `terraform get` command:

```
$> terraform get
Get: file:///home/kshirinkin/work/packt-terraform-
rewrites/modules/application
```

This created a symlink to your module inside the `.terraform` directory:

```
$> ls -la .terraform/modules
total 12
drwxr-xr-x. 2 kshirinkin kshirinkin 4096 Jan  3 16:08 .
drwxr-xr-x. 3 kshirinkin kshirinkin 4096 Jan  3 16:08 ..
lrwxrwxrwx. 1 kshirinkin kshirinkin   66 Jan  3 16:08
8a6e0ac9202efe2b1f0a69ae2d5138bb -> /home/kshirinkin/work/packt-terraform-
rewrites/modules/application
```

Resource Dependencies and Modules

You should be able to run the `terraform apply` command now. Let's add a second module, just to verify that we are still doing things right:

```
module "crazy_foods" {
  source = "./modules/application"
  vpc_id = "${aws_vpc.my_vpc.id}"
  subnet_id = "${aws_subnet.public.id}"
  name = "CrazyFoods"
}
```

Run the `terraform get` and `terraform plan` commands to check whether Terraform will do everything as expected, and pay attention to this part of the output:

```
+ module.mighty_trousers.aws_security_group.allow_http
    description:                "Allow HTTP traffic"
    name:                       "MightyTrousers allow_http"
```

> For non-local modules, in order to update the module, you need to pass the -update flag to the `terraform get` command: `terraform get -update`. Otherwise, the latest version of the module won't be downloaded.

Note how the name of the resource was built; it includes the module name and a `module` keyword. This doesn't mean that you can reference this module by this name though. Try to do it as follows:

```
module "crazy_foods" {
  source = "./modules/application"
  vpc_id = "${aws_vpc.my_vpc.id}"
  subnet_id = "${aws_subnet.public.id}"
  name = "CrazyFoods ${module.mighty_trousers.aws_security_group.allow_http.id}"
}
```

You will get an error saying * `module.crazy_foods: missing dependency: module.mighty_trousers.output.aws_security_group.allow_http.id`. You cannot simply reference resources inside a module from outside the module. You have to use outputs.

[59]

Retrieving module data with outputs

Another useful construct that Terraform provides are outputs. In an output, you define which data you want to be returned by the module. Add the following line to the very bottom of the `./modules/application/application.tf` file:

```
output "hostname" {
  value = "${aws_instance.app-server.private_dns}"
}
```

Now you can use this output inside the `template.tf` like this:

```
module "crazy_foods" {
  source = "./modules/application"
  vpc_id = "${aws_vpc.my_vpc.id}"
  subnet_id = "${aws_subnet.public.id}"
  name = "CrazyFoods ${module.mighty_trousers.hostname}"
}
```

Besides the obvious ability to get data from the module, there is another use case for module outputs: forcing dependencies. Here is the graph before passing the output to the second module:

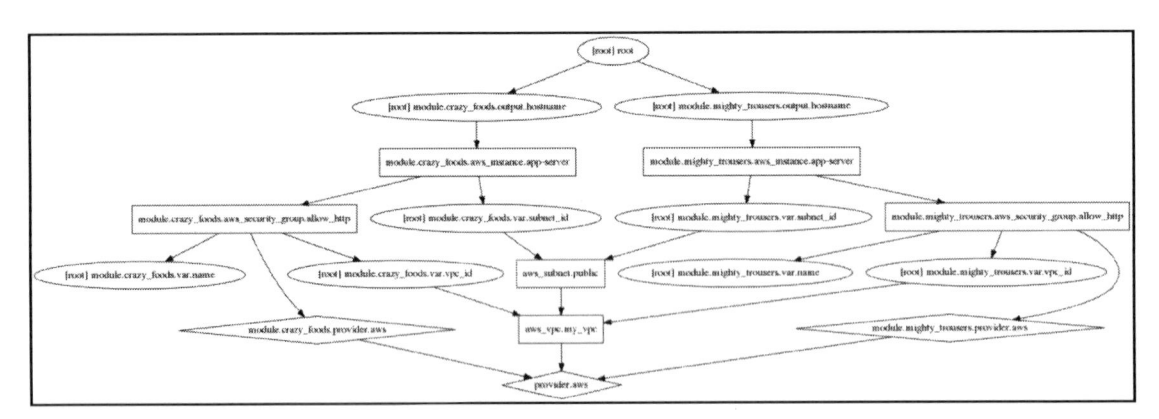

[60]

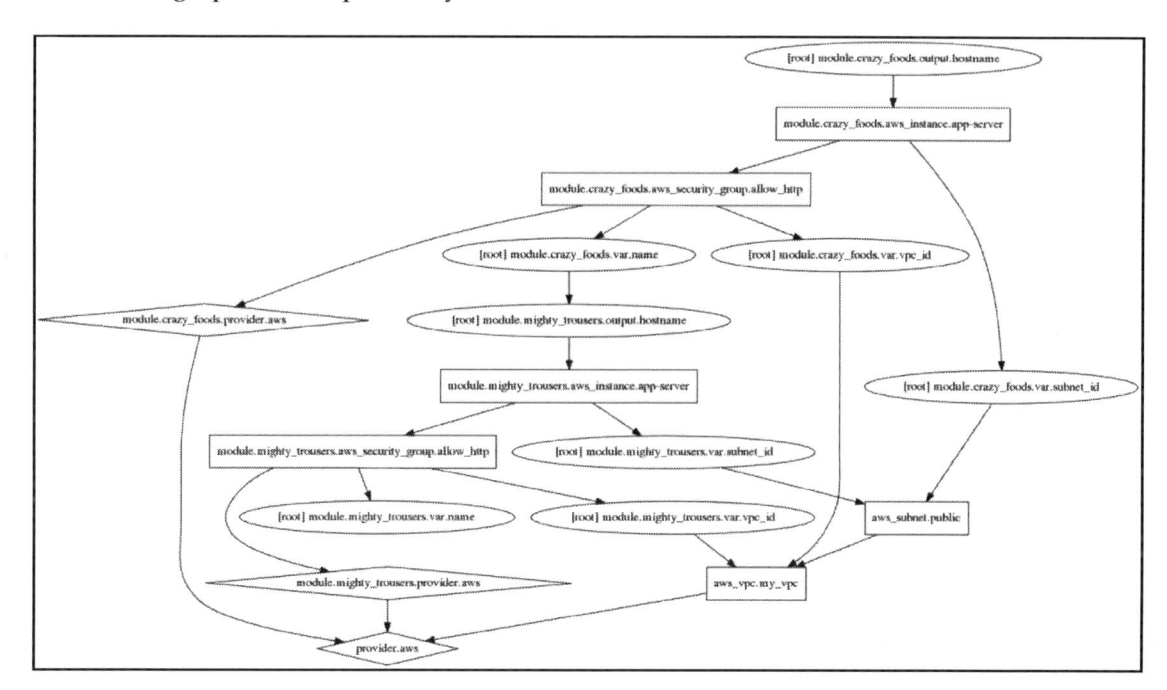

Here is the graph with dependency forced:

That's a completely different level of graph-beauty, I hope you agree. But sometimes, as we discussed previously, we have to do it. For example, one module creates a master server and the other one is responsible for slaves.

Since Terraform 0.8.0, you can specify a module inside the depends_on attribute. This will result to the resource dependant on all resources from the module. Prior to 0.8.0, you have to trick Terraform to do it with a combination of outputs and other trickery. Note that Terraform still doesn't allow a module to depend on another module directly via depends_on--this attribute is not available for modules whatsoever.

Using root module outputs

We already know that even our template.tf file is a module, named root module. And as with any module, it also has outputs. There is a terraform output command that retrieves outputs from your configuration. You can use it with modules, as well as with the main template. Let's first create our *MightyTrousers* module with terraform apply (you can remove the *CrazyFoods* module from template.tf for now, just to avoid extra AWS costs).

After the application is complete, run the `terraform output` command with the module name specified:

```
$> terraform output -module=mighty_trousers hostname
ip-10-0-1-181.eu-central-1.compute.internal
```

As an exercise, add the output to `template.tf`, it will get its value from the module output, and try to retrieve it by simply running the `terraform output` hostname.

Outputs are a simple yet powerful way to connect Terraform with all kinds of different tools. For example, you could output a bastion host IP to your test suite. We will talk more about this and other ways of connecting Terraform with other tools in Chapter 5, *Connecting with Other Tools*.

Summary

In this chapter, we learned a few important concepts behind Terraform. We now know how Terraform leverages the power of graph theory to manage dependencies between resources, and saw how exactly it builds graphs via the `terraform graph` command. There were many graphs to look at, and with the help of them, we learned how Terraform allows you to add more flexibility to dependency handling via the `depends_on` and `ignore_changes` parameters.

After learning about this important backbone of Terraform, we started writing a slightly more mature template and soon figured out that it has some issues with code duplication. Luckily, we managed to use Terraform modules to reduce the duplication and, more importantly, we even found out that the very first template we wrote was already a module.

We even took a first look at variables! But now, the question is: how to configure Terraform modules and resources for real? How to supply configuration, where is it stored, and how to manage updates? These are questions we will get answers to in the next chapter.

4
Storing and Supplying Configuration

So far, we know how to codify our infrastructure into Terraform templates of varying sizes. We know how to structure templates and how to split and reuse them with modules. More than this, we have already figured out important concepts behind how Terraform works. But there is an important piece we have hardly looked at: **configuration**.

A template with only hardcoded data in it is a bad template. You can't reuse it in other projects without modifying it. You will always have to update it by hand if some value changes. And you have to store a lot of information that doesn't really belong to the infrastructure template.

In this chapter, we will learn how to make Terraform templates more configurable. First, we will take a `lookup` variables and all the possible ways to use them. Then, we will learn how to use data resources to retrieve information from outside Terraform template. Finally, we will use built-in provider's capabilities to generate random data, secrets, and config files. As a bonus, we will also take a very quick look at another HashiCorp tool: **Consul**.

Understanding variables

If you've ever used any programming language, then you might be familiar with **variables** already. In most common case, they allow you to assign a value (a number or string or something else) to some hand-picked name and reference this value by this name inside your code. If you need to modify the value, then you just need to do it once, in a place where variable is defined.

Storing and Supplying Configuration

Unlike in programming languages, variables in Terraform are more like input data for your templates: you define them before using the template. During the Terraform run, you have zero control over variables. The values of variables never change; you can't modify them inside the template.

In the previous chapter, we already tried variables in order to configure modules. We also learned that our `template.tf` is a module: **root module**. Let's define some variables for the root module.

It is a common pattern to split variables, template, and outputs into three different files. As you might remember, Terraform loads all files with the `.tf` extension from the current folder, so you don't need to do any extra steps to join these three files. Let's create a new file `variables.tf` with the following content:

```
variable "region" {}
```

Now let's use it inside `template.tf` to configure AWS provider:

```
provider "aws" {
  region = "${var.region}"
}
```

If we would try to apply or plan template now, Terraform would interactively ask us for the value of this variable:

```
$> terraform plan
var.region
  Enter a value:
```

That's nice and sometimes convenient, but in most cases, you don't want to type values of all variables every time. Not only it's inconvenient, but it could also be dangerous: mistyping a variable value can lead to terrible consequences. If one of the variables is used inside a resource parameter that causes its recreation, then mistyping it will lead to accidental removal of the resource. Don't rely on the manual input of configuration data.

We could reduce the chances of accidental infrastructure destruction by adding a description to the variable:

```
variable "region" {
  description = "AWS region. Changing it will lead to loss of complete stack."
}
```

Now the user of the template will see this description when he or she tries to apply it:

```
$> terraform plan
var.region
  AWS region. Changing it will lead to loss of complete stack.
  Enter a value:
```

It doesn't save us from typos though. What would be an even more reliable way to protect the infrastructure from human mistakes is to have a default value for the variable:

```
variable "region" {
  description = "AWS region. Changing it will lead to loss of complete stack."
  default = "eu-central-1"
}
```

With the default value in place, Terraform won't ask for the value interactively anymore. It will pick default value unless other sources of variables are present.

There are three types of variables you can set:

- the `string` variables (default ones)
- the `map` variables
- the `list` variables

You can only interactively set the `string` variables; for `map` and `list`, you have to use other methods, which we will take a look at a bit later.

Using map variables

If you've used maps, dictionaries, or hashes in some programming language such as Ruby, then you know what **Map** in Terraform is. Map is a `lookup` table, where you specify multiple keys with different values. You can then pick the value depending on the key. It's easier to understand it with the example.

At the moment our `MightyTrousers` application always uses the `t2.micro` instance type. These are cheap instances that are good for quick tests and development, but they are not that great for production. What we want, actually, is a way to use different instance types depending on the environment stack is deployed to. Let's assume that we have only three environments: `dev`, `prod`, and `test`.

Storing and Supplying Configuration

First, let's move variables out of the `modules/application/application.tf` file to `modules/application/variables.tf`. And then let's define two new variables there: `environment` and `instance_type`.

```
variable "environment" { default = "dev" }
variable "instance_type" {
  type = "map"
  default = {
    dev = "t2.micro"
    test = "t2.medium"
    prod = "t2.large"
  }
}
```

We specified `type` explicitly, even though it's not really required when we have the `default` value as well. The default type is `string`.

What you also need to do is to add `variable "environment"{default = "prod" }` to the `variables.tf` file in the `root` folder of our project. We will use `prod` on top level to show that root module variable value will override the default of module itself.

Then, modify the module to look as follows:

```
module "mighty_trousers" {
  source = "./modules/application"
  vpc_id = "${aws_vpc.my_vpc.id}"
  subnet_id = "${aws_subnet.public.id}"
  name = "MightyTrousers"
  environment = "${var.environment}"
}
```

Here, we pass a variable from the root module to the application module. We don't need to pass the `instance_type` variable because we will just look at the value we need from the existing variable. To do this, Terraform provides the `lookup()` interpolation function. This function accepts `map` as the first argument, the key to look for in this `map` as the second argument, and an optional default value as the third argument. Let's modify our `modules/application/application.tf` `aws_instance` resource to look as follows:

```
resource "aws_instance" "app-server" {
  ami = "ami-9bf712f4"
  instance_type = "${lookup(var.instance_type, var.environment)}"
  subnet_id = "${var.subnet_id}"
  vpc_security_group_ids = ["${aws_security_group.allow_http.id}"]
  tags {
```

```
    Name = "${var.name}"
  }
}
```

We did not specify the default value inside the `lookup()` function; there is already a default on both module and root levels. Let's run the `terraform plan` command to see which parameters the instance would get:

```
$> terraform plan
< .... >
+ module.mighty_trousers.aws_instance.app-server
    ami:                          "ami-378f925b"
    availability_zone:            "<computed>"
    ebs_block_device.#:           "<computed>"
    ephemeral_block_device.#:     "<computed>"
    instance_state:               "<computed>"
    instance_type:                "t2.large"
    key_name:                     "<computed>"
    network_interface_id:         "<computed>"
    placement_group:              "<computed>"
    private_dns:                  "<computed>"
    private_ip:                   "<computed>"
    public_dns:                   "<computed>"
    public_ip:                    "<computed>"
    root_block_device.#:          "<computed>"
    security_groups.#:            "<computed>"
    source_dest_check:            "true"
    subnet_id:                    "${var.subnet_id}"
    tags.%:                       "1"
    tags.Name:                    "MightyTrousers"
    tenancy:                      "<computed>"
    vpc_security_group_ids.#:     "<computed>"
```

Indeed it took the `t2.large` instance type. Maps give you more flexibility compared with regular string variables. So create lists.

Using list variables

Continuing analogy with programming, `list` in Terraform is similar to arrays in most programming languages. There is a very nice place where we can use lists in our templates: **security group**.

Storing and Supplying Configuration

Currently, an application module defines a single security group and assigns it to the instance. But an EC2 instance can have multiple security groups attached. We could have a default security group that allows an SSH access and then on an application level we have another one for app-specific permissions.

Let's add yet another variable to `module/application/variables.tf`, with an empty list as a default value:

```
variable "extra_sgs" { default = [] }
```

Now, let's define a default security group in `template.tf` with SSH access allowed:

```
resource "aws_security_group" "default" {
  name = "Default SG"
  description = "Allow SSH access"
  vpc_id = "${aws_vpc.my_vpc.id}"

  ingress {
    from_port = 22
    to_port = 22
    protocol = "tcp"
    cidr_blocks = ["0.0.0.0/0"]
  }
}
```

Now we can pass it to the module, wrapping it with square brackets (which means it's a list):

```
module "mighty_trousers" {
  source = "./modules/application"
  vpc_id = "${aws_vpc.my_vpc.id}"
  subnet_id = "${aws_subnet.public.id}"
  name = "MightyTrousers"
  environment = "${var.environment}"
  extra_sgs = ["${aws_security_group.default.id}"]
}
```

Now we only need to use this extra security group ID together with an app-specific security group. To achieve this, we will use the `concat()` interpolation function. This function joins multiple lists into one. We also better ensure that the resulting list doesn't have duplicates. The `distinct()` function will help with this; it removes all the duplicates, keeping only the first occurrence of each non-unique element. We will join the `extra_sgs` list with a list made from an app-specific SG defined in `application.tf`:

```
resource "aws_instance" "app-server" {
  ami = "ami-9bf712f4"
  instance_type = "${lookup(var.instance_type, var.environment)}"
```

```
    subnet_id = "${var.subnet_id}"
    vpc_security_group_ids = ["${distinct(concat(var.extra_sgs,
  aws_security_group.allow_http.*.id))}"]
    tags {
      Name = "${var.name}"
    }
  }
```

The syntax might not look obvious here, especially if you come from programming background. It takes some time to get used to peculiarities of Terraform DSL. One would expect that because we have a single app-specific security group, we would simply wrap it with square brackets as follows:

```
["${concat(var.extra_sgs, [aws_security_group.allow_http.id]}"]
```

Unfortunately, it doesn't work like this. Internally, we defined that `aws_security_group` is not a single resource, but a list consists of a single resource. Terraform doesn't have loops. Instead, it has a special syntax to iterate over the multiple resources with the * symbol. In the background, we have the following:

```
aws_security_group.allow_http.*.id
```

Terraform transforms the preceding into something similar to the following:

```
[aws_security_group.allow_http.0.id]
```

Let's say we would have multiple groups that would result in the following:

```
[aws_security_group.allow_http.0.id .. aws_security_group.allow_http.N.id]
```

Here, N is the number of groups. We haven't discussed how to create multiple instances of the same resource yet, though. That's the topic for another chapter.

> Terraform language can be very confusing at times. Since version 0.8.0, there is a `terraform console` command, which allows you to play around with different interpolation functions and other features in an interactive console. The console itself is quite unpredictable as well, but you should expect it to become more useful over time.

Both map and list allow building complex though sometimes not obvious constructions around Terraform variables via various interpolation function's usage. But so far, we have still defined our variables only via default values. It's time to figure out how to do it differently. First, let's learn how to provide variable values inline with Terraform commands invocation.

Supplying variables inline

The easiest (after interactive mode) way to set variable values is to specify them as an argument to Terraform command. It's done with the multiple -var arguments to the command with the name and value of the variable following:

```
$> terraform plan -var 'environment=dev'
```

Note how instance type of the EC2 server is different because we set the variable environment to dev.

So far, we don't have any map or list variables for the root module. Let's add a list of CIDR blocks that are allowed to access default security group via SSH. Also, let's add map with CIDR blocks for our subnets. We will have two blocks: for private and for public subnets accordingly. In the end, variables.tf should look as follows:

```
variable "region" {
  description = "AWS region. Changing it will lead to loss of complete stack."
  default = "eu-central-1"
}
variable "environment" { default = "prod" }
variable "allow_ssh_access" {
  description = "List of CIDR blocks that can access instances via SSH"
  default = ["0.0.0.0/0"]
}
variable "vpc_cidr" { default = "10.0.0.0/16" }
variable "subnet_cidrs" {
  description = "CIDR blocks for public and private subnets"
  default = {
    public = "10.0.1.0/24"
    private = "10.0.2.0/24"
  }
}
```

As an exercise, make use of these new variables yourself with the help of the lookup() function.

If we tried to supply the allow_ssh_access variable via command line, it would look like this:

```
$> terraform plan -var 'allow_ssh_access=["52.123.123.123/32"]'
```

If we needed to change CIDR blocks' `map`, then we could do it as follows:

```
$> terraform plan -var 'subnet_cidrs={public = "172.0.16.0/24", private = "172.0.17.0/24"}'
```

Setting variables via CLI arguments can be useful sometimes: to provide a password for some service or to tweak some values for development purposes. But it is in no way a reliable and production-ready storage. There is a better option: **environment variables**.

Using Terraform environment variables

The third way (after interactive input and inline arguments) to supply values to your variables is to use environment variables.

> The environment variables are part of the environment where process is running and the program can access them. There are always some environment variables already set; for example, `$PATH` defines paths where your shell will look for executables. You can get a list of currently set environment variables with the `env` command on *nix operating systems.

Terraform will automatically read all environment variables with the `TF_VAR_` prefix. For example, to set value for the `region` variable, you would need to set the `TF_VAR_region` environment variable.

There are multiple ways to set environment variables. You could do it inline with your `terraform` command execution, as follows:

```
$> TF_VAR_region=eu-central-1 terraform plan
```

But that's not much different from setting variables with the `-var` argument. Alternatively, you could set them once in your terminal:

```
$> export TF_VAR_subnet_cidrs='{public = "172.0.16.0/24", private = "172.0.17.0/24"}'
$> terraform plan
```

This would set the variable value for the current terminal session. You could unset it with the `unset` command:

```
$> unset TF_VAR_subnet_cidrs
```

Storing and Supplying Configuration

It might be tempting to set all variables with `export`, but it can cause some problems: you don't have an easy overview of which variable has which value.

> A quick way to check which terraform variables are defined via environment variables on **nix* operating systems is to run `env | grep "TF_VAR"`.

Of course, you could store your environment variables inside a text file and source it. Create a file `vars` with the following contents:

```
export TF_VAR_subnet_cidrs='{public = "172.0.16.0/24", private = "172.0.17.0/24"}'
export TF_VAR_region=eu-central-1
```

Then, `source` this file to make it available in your environment:

```
$> source vars
$> terraform plan
```

This approach still doesn't prevent you from reassigning an environment variable by accident. Once again, environment variables are good for development, but it's not the best solution yet. An even better way is to use **variable files**.

Using variable files

When running Terraform commands, you can optionally supply a variable file via the -var-file argument. The syntax of these files is the good old HCL, familiar to you from Terraform templates themselves. Create a new file named `development.tfvars` and set your variables there:

```
region = "eu-central-1"
vpc_cidr = "172.0.0.0/16"
subnet_cidrs = {
  public = "172.0.16.0/24"
  private = "172.0.17.0/24"
}
```

To use it, run `terraform plan` command with `-var-file` argument:

```
$> terraform plan -var-file=./development.tfvars
```

Storing and Supplying Configuration

It's much more reliable to use variable files for production stacks: you always know which values are there and you can store them in version control. And for sensitive things, such as a personal password to access the cloud account, you would still use environment variables or inline arguments.

> In `Chapter 7`, *Collaborative Infrastructure*, we will discuss better ways to deal with sensitive data.

To go one step even further, you could remove all defaults from `variables.tf` and set them only in the `variable` file, to completely eliminate configuration from your template.

> You could supply multiple variable files, with the ones defined later taking precedence over the ones defined earlier.

Variables are the first-class configuration in Terraform. With a set of simple but flexible ways to use and set them, you have a full control over how to create your environment. For production use, variable files are a must. You can write them yourself or use a script that fetches remote data and generates a variable file.

Variables are not the only source of configuration though. Since Terraform 0.7, there are data sources as well. Let's take a look at why and how we can use them.

Configuring data sources

Data sources are very similar to regular resources. The main difference is that they are *read-only*. You can't always (actually, far from it) have the complete infrastructure in your Terraform templates. It is often the case that some resources already exist and you don't have much control over them. You still need to use them inside your Terraform templates, though. That's when data sources become handy.

In the Terraform documentation for each provider, there is a list of data sources (if any are available). They are configured almost the same as regular resources, with some differences.

Let's try them out in our template. There is a feature named **VPC Peering** in AWS. It allows the connection of two different VPCs in a way that instances inside both can talk to each other. We could have a VPC provided by another team, responsible for management layer for our infrastructure (artifacts storage, DNS, and so on). In order to access it from VPC we created with Terraform, we need to set up peering.

Storing and Supplying Configuration

> You could peer VPCs in two different AWS accounts. But we will peer two VPCs in a single AWS account for demonstration purposes.

First, create a new VPC manually via AWS management console as shown in the following screenshot:

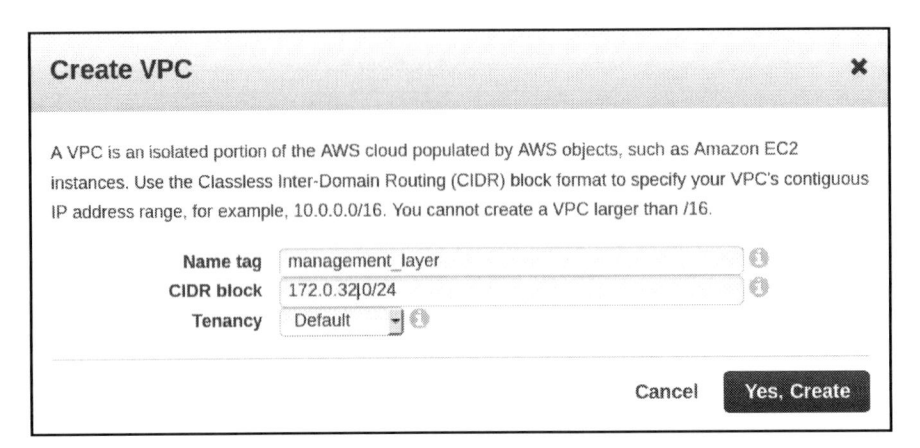

Create VPC

A VPC is an isolated portion of the AWS cloud populated by AWS objects, such as Amazon EC2 instances. Use the Classless Inter-Domain Routing (CIDR) block format to specify your VPC's contiguous IP address range, for example, 10.0.0.0/16. You cannot create a VPC larger than /16.

- Name tag: management_layer
- CIDR block: 172.0.32.0/24
- Tenancy: Default

Cancel   Yes, Create

Then copy the ID of following VPC:

management_layer   vpc-ace803c4   available   172.0.32.0/24   dopt-b82bc8d1   rtb-8a5199e2   acl-96418cfe   Default

Now we are ready to use VPC data source. Add it to your template, before creating our old VPC:

```
data "aws_vpc" "management_layer" {
  id = "vpc-c36cbdab"
}
```

Of course, you need to replace VPC ID with the one you've created manually. Now we can create a peering connection between manually-created VPC and Terraform-created VPC:

```
data "aws_vpc" "management_layer" {
  id = "vpc-c36cbdab"
}

resource "aws_vpc" "my_vpc" {
  cidr_block = "${var.vpc_cidr}"
}

resource "aws_vpc_peering_connection" "my_vpc-management" {
```

```
    peer_vpc_id = "${data.aws_vpc.management_layer.id}"
    vpc_id = "${aws_vpc.my_vpc.id}"
    auto_accept = true
}
```

Data sources are referenced with the `data` keyword in front of resource name.

That's not the most sophisticated example of data sources, as you might have noted: we could simply use management layer VPC ID directly, without data sources at all. There is, perhaps, a better example: fetching AMI ID's via data source.

AMI (Amazon Machine Image) is an image format used on AWS. It's a starting point for each EC2 instance. There are many publicly available AMIs for different operating systems, sometimes with software already preinstalled and preconfigured (such as Wordpress).

AWS users can create their own AMIs with the process widely named as **image baking**. The simplest way to bake an image is first to create a new instance from existing AMI, then configure it (manually or with some configuration management tool) and make a new AMI out of this instance.

Some companies take this process to extreme levels by baking tons of AMIs every day and recreating existing instances with new AMIs, instead of performing in-place upgrades. This approach enables you to achieve so-called **immutable infrastructure**, where you never touch a running server at all and each update is performed by recreating an instance. We will learn how to create an immutable infrastructure with Terraform in Chapter 6, *Scaling and Updating Infrastructure*.

HashiCorp tools, including Terraform, are often built with immutable infrastructure approach in mind. Packer, another product of this company, is focused exactly on creating images for multiple platforms. We are going to discuss how to orchestrate these kind of upgrades with Terraform in a later chapter. But in this chapter, let's use AMI data source inside application module to fetch an AMI for our EC2 instance:

```
data "aws_ami" "app-ami" {
  most_recent = true
  owners = ["self"]
}

resource "aws_instance" "app-server" {
  ami = "${data.aws_ami.app-ami.id}"
  instance_type = "${lookup(var.instance_type, var.environment)}"
  subnet_id = "${var.subnet_id}"
  vpc_security_group_ids = ["${concat(var.extra_sgs,
aws_security_group.allow_http.*.id)}"]
  tags {
```

Storing and Supplying Configuration

```
        Name = "${var.name}"
    }
}
```

This code will pull most recently created AMI from the AWS account used for Terraform runs. We don't even need to know the ID; it will be retrieved automatically. For sure we shouldn't fetch most recent AMI all the time, but it can break the environment if most recent AMI is wrong. But then, of course, Terraform allows you to be more specific about which AMI to fetch using filters and regular expressions inside this data source. We will omit the usage of them and leave it as an exercise.

Data sources are relatively new concept in Terraform, and there are still not that many of them, especially for third-party providers, developed by community. Some of data sources might look almost useless, whereas others provide a handy way to retrieve remote data to use inside the template.

There are two particularly useful data sources that needs further discussion:

- `template_file`
- `external_file`

Providing configuration with template_file

It's not an unusual situation when you need to provide long-form non-Terraform-specific text configuration to your Terraform templates. On many occasions, you need to pass to Terraform a bootstrap script for your virtual machines, or upload large file to S3, or, another example, configure IAM policies.

Sometimes, these files are static, that is, you don't need to change anything inside them, you just need to read their contents inside Terraform template. For this use case, there is a `file()` function. You pass a relative path to your file as an argument to this function, and it will read its contents to whatever place you need.

Let's use this function to upload a public SSH key to EC2. Add the following snippet to `template.tf`, right before an application module:

```
resource "aws_key_pair" "terraform" {
  key_name = "terraform"
  public_key = "${file("./id_rsa.pub")}"
}
```

Storing and Supplying Configuration

You need to either copy existing public key to your working directory or generate new one with the `ssh-keygen` command. As an exercise, use this key pair when creating an application EC2 instance in order to get SSH access to it with your private key.

If you are a heavy IAM user, then you might want to create extra directory *policies* in your Terraform directory, where you could store all your `json` definitions of policies. Then, creating a policy could look as simple as:

```
resource "aws_iam_role_policy" "s3-assets-all" {
  name = "s3=assets@all"
  role = "${aws_iam_role.app-production.id}"
  policy = "${file("policies/s3=assets@all.json")}"
}
```

AWS doesn't provide a convenient way to reuse and version policies. With Terraform, you can easily have both.

> As mentioned in `Chapter 1`, *Infrastructure Automation*, it is critical to have a solid naming scheme for everything you do in the cloud. In the earlier S3 policy snippet, one possible naming scheme is used: policy name is built as `${service_name}=${resource_name}@${action_name}`. This makes the whole policies usage much cleaner.

Static files as a preceding public key example are common, but sometimes, you need more control over the contents of your files. Terraform provides the `template_file` data source, responsible for rendering text templates. It's really useful for bootstrap scripts, such as the ones you provide to `cloud-init`.

So far, we haven't done much of configuration of the EC2 instance we've created. Let's install some packages on it and then configure additional DNS server. We will set a DNS server as a variable for a root module and pass it down to the application module. We will also add an extra variable for packages to be installed for this module.

First, let's define new variables in `variables.tf`:

```
variable "external_nameserver" { default = "8.8.8.8" }
variable "extra_packages" {
  description = "Additional packages to install for particular module"
  default = {
    MightyTrousers = "wget bind-utils"
  }
}
```

[77]

Storing and Supplying Configuration

Note how `map` is used here: one key per specific application. There is no way in Terraform to pass variables directly to modules. If you want to configure something in module, you need to define similar variable for the root module and then pass it to the module. Unfortunately, this means that you need to duplicate every variable: once in the root module, and then in the module you want to configure.

The problem comes when you reuse the same module multiple times, for example, to set up multiple different applications. In this case, multiple approaches can be used. You could prefix a variable name with a module instance name:

```
variable "mighty_trousers_extra_packages" { }
```

Or you could use maps and then `lookup` value you need. Using maps provides better grouping of variables, and it's easier to set default value:

```
variable "extra_packages" {
  description = "Additional packages to install for particular module"
  default = {
    base = "wget"
    MightyTrousers = "wget bind-utils"
  }
}
```

Then, when you pass this variable to module, you can always fall back to default:

```
"${lookup(var.extra_packages, "my_app", "base")}"
```

Let's pass the `add` variables to the module at the bottom of the `modules/application/variables.tf` file:

```
variable "extra_packages" {}
variable "external_nameserver" {}
```

At this point, it might be unclear when and where to specify default values for variables. We did specify them in a root module, but did not do it in application module. If we always pass variables from the top level to the module level, then there is no real need for defaults on the module level; defaults from the top will set values for the module. But if in some cases, we do not pass variables to module from the root module, then defaults for module variables are required. It depends on how you use and configure your modules.

In general, when it comes to configuring modules, current Terraform APIs to do it can seem a bit fragile and inflexible. You can easily end up with lots of duplication and a bit of a mess when it comes to finding the source of truth for variable values. It might become more robust in future Terraform releases, of course. But as of version 0.8, one needs to take these limitations into consideration.

We are finally ready to use template file data source. Add it to `modules/application/application.tf`:

```
data "template_file" "user_data" {
  template = "${file("${path.module}/user_data.sh.tpl")}"

  vars {
    packages = "${var.extra_packages}"
    nameserver = "${var.external_nameserver}"
  }
}
```

The `template_file` allows the passing of variables to the file, thus giving you a chance to configure this file with some specific values. The file itself is specified as a `template` parameter. Note the use of `${path.module}`: by default path will be relative to the root template files. `${path.module}` allows you to use the path to the module folder without guessing it.

Create a file `modules/application/user_data.sh.tpl` with the following content:

```
#!/usr/bin/bash
yum install ${packages} -y
echo "${nameserver}" >> /etc/resolv.conf
```

Variables inside template files are used pretty much the same way they are used in Terraform templates. You need to be careful, though: dollar sign is used in both Terraform and regular `bash` scripts. Sometimes, you will have to escape the dollar sign, so Terraform doesn't try to interpolate it and therefore doesn't fail. Escaping is done simply by duplicating dollar sign: `$$`.

Finally, let's render this template file as a user data for the instance:

```
resource "aws_instance" "app-server" {
  ami = "${data.aws_ami.app-ami.id}"
  instance_type = "${lookup(var.instance_type, var.environment)}"
  subnet_id = "${var.subnet_id}"
  vpc_security_group_ids = ["${concat(var.extra_sgs,
aws_security_group.allow_http.*.id)}"]
  user_data = "${data.template_file.user_data.rendered}"
  tags {
    Name = "${var.name}"
  }
}
```

Storing and Supplying Configuration

Now, if we got the script right, after EC2 instance will be created, `cloud-init` will run this script and extra packages and the new external `nameserver` will be configured.

Changing `user_data` normally leads to resource recreation. We don't really want our server to be destroyed when this file changes. Let's revise what we learned in previous chapter about life cycle block and tell the instance to ignore changes of `user_data`:

```
lifecycle {
  ignore_changes = ["user_data"]
}
```

Template files provide an easy way to generate bigger configuration files that can later be reused in order to set up the machines, external services, and so on. For `cloud-init`, use-case Terraform also provides the `template_cloud_init_config` resource that renders multipart `cloud-init` config from source files.

A template file is not the only provider that is useful for configuration purposes. Let's take a quick look at few other resources that Terraform provides.

Providing data from anywhere with external_data

As of Terraform 0.8, there is also an `external_data` resource. It allows us to call any other program and use the data returned by it, as long as it implements a specific protocol. The main requirement for this program is that it returns a valid JSON as a result of execution. Create the following tiny Ruby script in the root template directory:

```
require 'json'
data = {
  owner: "Packt"
}
puts data.to_json
```

> You need to have Ruby installed for this to work.

Now configure external data resource as follows:

```
data "external" "example" {
  program = ["ruby", "${path.module}/custom_data_source.rb"]
}
```

Finally, use it inside the module to extend its name attribute:

```
module "mighty_trousers" {
  source = "./modules/application"
  vpc_id = "${aws_vpc.my_vpc.id}"
  subnet_id = "${aws_subnet.public.id}"
  name = "MightyTrousers-${data.external.example.result.owner}"
  # ...
}
```

As you see, you can access any JSON object key via the `result` attribute of external data source. As of Terraform version 0.8.2, it is not possible to use nested keys from the result, it is limited to the flat objects.

An external data source is an extremely powerful resource. Essentially, it allows you to connect absolutely any data source to your Terraform templates - third party APIs, SQL databases, NoSQL databases, you name it. You just need to implement a tiny wrapper between Terraform and this data source to comply with what Terraform expects. You could even connect Terraform to the data storage of your configuration management tool, be it Puppet Hiera, Puppet DB, or Chef APIs.

Note, though, that using this resource you need to ensure that every machine that uses this template has all the software used inside external data source program - Terraform won't do that for you. In the previously mentioned example, you need to make sure that Terraform users have Ruby installed. That's also the reason why Terraform Enterprise can't guarantee that your template will work well when it has this data source; you cannot expect Terraform Enterprise to have any extra software installed.

Remove the external data source from our root template. There are some more resources that give you a bit more flexibility in terms of configuring your templates. Let's explore them.

Exploring Terraform configuration resources

Quite frequently, you will require some random data to be generated. This could be default password for a database or a random `hostname` for your servers. Terraform has random provider that solves this problem.

Storing and Supplying Configuration

Of course, completely random values are harmful for Terraform. That's why, the `random_id` resource generates random string only on creation and then value is kept during updates (unless you change the configuration of this resource). Imagine that we want to pass random `hostname` to the previously configured `template_file` user data. We could do it as follows:

```
resource "random_id" "hostname" {
  byte_length = 4
}
data "template_file" "user_data" {
  template = "${file("${path.module}/user_data.sh.tpl")}"
  vars {
    packages = "${var.extra_packages}"
    nameserver = "${var.external_nameserver}"
    hostname = "${random_id.hostname.b64}"
  }
}
```

Then, the actual script can use the `hostname` variable to set the `hostname` of the machine. If you want to have more control over when exactly `random_id` is recreated (and thus value is regenerated), then you can specify `keepers` parameter. `keepers` are stored in `map`, and when value of one of the keys is changed, then random value is regenerated. For example, take a look at the AMI ID `keepers`:

```
resource "random_id" "hostname" {
  keepers {
    ami_id = "${data.aws_ami.app-ami.id}"
  }
  byte_length = 4
}
```

Thus, if new AMI is there, then instance will be recreated and new hostname will be required.

In addition, there is a `random_shuffle` resource that will return a randomly ordered list of items from the original list you provided. You could even use it together with the `hostname` generator we saw in the preceding example:

```
resource "random_shuffle" "hostname_creature" {
  input = ["griffin", "gargoyle", "dragon"]
  result_count = 1
}
resource "random_id" "hostname_random" {
  byte_length = 4
}
data "template_file" "user_data" {
```

Storing and Supplying Configuration

```
      template = "${file("${path.module}/user_data.sh.tpl")}"

    vars {
      packages = "${var.extra_packages}"
      nameserver = "${var.external_nameserver}"
      hostname =
"${random_shuffle.hostname_creature.result[0]}${random_id.hostname.b64}"
    }
  }
```

That's the complete random hostnames generator in a handful of lines of code right there!

Another important Terraform provider we will most probably requires is a TLS provider. The resources of this provider are used to generate Transport Layer Security keys and certificates. It's a very handy way to generate few secret keys though you must keep in mind that they will end up in your `state` file. Because of this, Terraform authors themselves do not recommend using it for production deployment

There are four resources you can use, as follows:

- `tls_private_key`
- `tls_self_signed_cert`
- `tls_locally_signed_cert`
- `tls_cert_request`

Their usage is well-documented in official Terraform documentation; let's just take a look at simplest one:

```
    resource "tls_private_key" "example" {
        algorithm = "ECDSA"
        ecdsa_curve = "P384"
    }
```

It will generate both private and public key and you could use it to get an initial SSH connection to the server.

As we know, the number of providers and resources in Terraform is growing fast and not all of them are purely external service providers. There is a still small set of useful providers to generate some data. There are not that many ways to attach more powerful configuration stores, though. Well, except for the one: **Consul**.

Taking a quick look at Consul

If we just count stars on GitHub, then Consul is probably the most popular HashiCorp tool. It's one of the few service discovery tools on the market and probably the only one that can be considered modern. The closest alternatives are ZooKeeper and **etcd**. ZooKeeper is known for being hard to set up and maintain and for being kind of too slow (written in Java) and old already (and you don't want to use anything older than few years these days, do you?). The etcd, though, is a very popular choice, lacks most of the features required for service discovery, and is just a storage rather than a complete solution.

Consul is both service discovery tool and a key/value storage. You need to install **Consul agent** on each node in order to get it working. As Consul is written in Go, the installation is not very complex: drop the binary and few configuration files to the server and configure system service (`systemd`, upstart or whatever you prefer) to run it. No other prerequisites are required. In addition, you need to have multiple **Consul masters**: each Consul agent will join the **Consul cluster** by connecting to each.

Once you have a cluster running, you can define services on your nodes via simple JSON configuration. For each service, there could be health checks, making sure that, for example, database is still available at a certain port. There is also a way to trigger events inside Consul cluster, there is an API to access Consul, and, most importantly, all of this is baked by key/value store and gossip protocol (provided by Serf--backbone of Consul and also a tool from HashiCorp). All these things together allow you to build systems that react to changes very quickly and that are easily discoverable. Consul can even replace internal DNS because it has a DNS server built in.

> Actually, Consul has many features and different usecases, and this fact kind of violates HashiCorp philosophy of buildings tools that solve one problem and solve it very well. But in this case, being an exception is good because all Consul features fit really nicely together and managing them as separate utilities would be rather inconvenient. Achieving the same result with etcd, for example, would require a couple of extra tools, at least.

Consul might not be the most sophisticated data storage, especially for huge amounts of data. But it is perfect for small sets of configuration, such as aforementioned services and health checks. You can easily write your own data to this storage, via API, for example.

If you are using both Terraform and Consul, it makes a lot of sense to connect them together. There is a Consul `provider` for Terraform that allows you to create Consul services, nodes, keys, and so on. More importantly, it has a data source `consul_keys`. With this data source, you can fetch any data from your Consul cluster, which means that you get a real data backend for your templates. It's up to you what you are going to store there and how you are going to use it, but here are few examples:

- AMI IDs for a particular instance type (`app-a` AMI, `db` AMI, and so on)
- Retrieve a list of nodes to be load balanced with Elastic Load Balancer
- Find the database replica for a particular AWS region

We are not going to set up the complete Consul cluster as it is really out of scope of this book. Nevertheless, let's look at a small example of using `consul_keys` to set the AMI instead of using data source for AMI:

```
provider "consul" {
    address = "consul.example.com:80"
    datacenter = "frankfurt"
}
data "consul_keys" "amis" {
    # Read the launch AMI from Consul
    key {
        name = "mighty_trousers"
        path = "ami"
    }
}
resource "aws_instance" "app-server" {
  ami = "${consul_keys.amis.var.mighty_trousers}"
  instance_type = "${lookup(var.instance_type, var.environment)}"
  subnet_id = "${var.subnet_id}"
  vpc_security_group_ids = ["${concat(var.extra_sgs,
aws_security_group.allow_http.*.id)}"]
  user_data = "${data.template_file.user_data.rendered}"
  tags {
    Name = "${var.name}"
  }
}
```

Consul is a powerful data backend for Terraform and, also being a product of HashiCorp, they are more likely to work nicely together. Consul can also be used as storage for state files, which we will discuss in later chapters. Other data backends might (and probably will) appear in future, but we should seriously consider Consul at least because of it being the part of the same technology stack.

Summary

There's been a lot of information in this chapter, but we finally know all the possible ways to supply configuration to Terraform templates. Let's recap what you learned.

You learned how to use variables in Terraform: what kind of variables we can use and how we can provide them interactively, inline, with environment variables and variable files. We also discovered data sources: a relatively new concept in Terraform that allows us to get read-only data. While perhaps being still a bit too new, we found few applications for this concept. Then, you learned how to generate configuration files with the `template_file` data source and on top of that, explored multiple other providers, all simplifying our configuration efforts. In the end, we even took a brief look into what Consul is and how it works with Terraform.

But Consul is not the only tool that you will want to use with Terraform. As Terraform is just a one utility in your infrastructure toolchain, you might be wondering how to connect it with other software. For example, how to connect it with configuration management tools? How to perform complex provisioning of servers? How to execute scripts after or during Terraform runs? In the next chapter, you will learn everything about connecting Terraform with other software.

5
Connecting with Other Tools

Even though Terraform is a great tool to describe your **Infrastructure as Code (IaC)**, it still covers only the highest level components of your system. It is perfect when you need to create cloud resources. It's especially hard to replace Terraform when your company relies on many AWS (or other large cloud provider) services. However, it is not the only tool you need for your infrastructure. HashiCorp makes it clear in the Tao of HashiCorp:

> *The simple, modular, composable approach allows us to build products at a higher level of abstraction. Rather than solving the holistic problem, we break it down into constituent parts, and solve those. We build the best possible solution for the scope of each problem, and then combine the blocks to form a solid, full solution.* - https://www.hashicorp.com/blog/tao-of-hashicorp.html

In this chapter, you will learn how to connect Terraform with other tools, most importantly with configuration management systems: how to make it play well with Ansible, Chef, and Puppet, how to bootstrap your machines properly, and how to invoke basically any other tool that you need to support your infrastructure. You will learn some new tools, such as testing frameworks and wrappers around Terraform state files. We will also take a sneak peek into a plugin system of Terraform.

Returning data with outputs

We've already talked very briefly about outputs in previous chapters. By this time, you should already know what they are. However, let's recap their usage anyway.

Outputs allow the returning of data from the Terraform template after it was applied using the `terraform output` command. For example, to return the IP address of an EC2 instance, we could define an output as follows:

```
output "public_ip" {
    value = "${aws_instance.web-server.public_ip}"
}
```

That allows us to easily pass this data to other scripts and tools. For example, with this approach, we could run tests against our servers. Enter **Inspec**.

Testing servers with Inspec

Just as your application, code should be covered by unit and integration tests. Infrastructure as code should have good test coverage as well. There are multiple ways to do infrastructure code tests. They are as follows:

- Test only the code, without creating a real infrastructure (with tools such as ChefSpec and rspec-puppet)
- Test a single server
- Test the complete system

We won't look at the first option to test our infrastructure in this book. For guidance on how to test the complete system (with all the cloud resources, servers, and so on), look at Chapter 7, *Collaborative Infrastructure*. As for this chapter, let's check one way to test a single server with Terraform and Inspec.

Inspec is a testing framework written in Ruby. It provides an *easy-to-understand* DSL that allows you to write human-readable descriptions of what the server should run, which packages it should have, and so on. The only thing Inspec needs is the address of the server. But, first things first: let's install Inspec.

Inspec is a Ruby gem, so you need to have Ruby installed on your system. Depending on your operating system, it could be either already installed or available via a package manager (`yum`, `dnf`, `apt-get`, `homebrew`, and so on). Once Ruby is installed, installing Inspec is just one command away:

```
$> gem install inspec
```

Connecting with Other Tools

Let's write a test that will check that the `wget` package is installed. Create a new folder `specs/`, and place a file named `base_spec.rb` inside of it with the following contents:

```
describe package('wget') do
  it { should be_installed }
end
```

> For the complete documentation on Inspec, consult the official website `http://inspec.io/`.

The only thing that prevents us from running this test is the missing IP address of the instance. And that's where Terraform will help us. First, update `./modules/application/application.tf` to have the output defined at the very button:

```
output "public_ip" {
  value = "${aws_instance.app-server.public_ip}"
}
```

Accordingly, add an output to the root `template.tf` file:

```
output "mighty_trousers_public_ip" {
  value = "${module.mighty_trousers.public_ip}"
}
```

In order for the instance to actually receive the public IP automatically, the subnet needs to have a special option enabled. Modify the `aws_subnet.public` resource to enable `map_public_ip_on_launch`:

```
resource "aws_subnet" "public" {
  vpc_id = "${aws_vpc.my_vpcmy_vpc.id}"
  cidr_block = "${lookup(var.subnet_cidrs, "public")}"
  map_public_ip_on_launch = true
}
```

> **TIP**: You can remove all VPC peering code from your template; we won't need it anymore.

Connecting with Other Tools

And now apply the template, as you've done so many times by now:

```
$> terraform apply
```

Give EC2 some time to completely set up the instance with `cloud-init` (remember, we are passing the custom `cloud-init` script generated with the `template_file` data resource). Then, run the test we wrote earlier:

```
$> inspec exec specs/base_spec.rb -t ssh://centos@$
(terraform output mighty_trousers_public_ip)-i ~/.ssh/id_rsa
```

Here, `~/.ssh/id_rsa` is used to connect to the server. Change it to point to the private key of a key pair you generated for Terraform.

The test will fail because we forgot to configure routing and add an internet gateway for our VPC. Currently, none of the instances can talk to the internet or be connected from the internet. The internet gateway is responsible for enabling internet connectivity inside VPC. Let's add it to `template.tf`:

```
resource "aws_internet_gateway" "gw" {
  vpc_id = "${aws_vpc.my_vpc.id}"
}
```

Then, modify a default route table to have routing to the outside world:

```
resource "aws_default_route_table" "default_routing" {
  default_route_table_id = "${aws_vpc.my_vpc.default_route_table_id}"
  route {
    cidr_block = "0.0.0.0/0"
    gateway_id = "${aws_internet_gateway.gw.id}"
  }
}
```

> There is always a default route table in AWS. Terraform provides the `aws_default_route_table` resource to give an easy way to update it. Otherwise, you would have to create it from scratch.

Apply the template and try to run Inspec again! You will get a bunch of error messages again, this time looking similar to the following:

```
INFO -- : [SSH] connection failed, retrying in 1 seconds
(#<Net::SSH::AuthenticationFailed: Authentication failed for user
centos@52.57.35.13>)
```

Remember that we created a key pair in the previous chapter? Well, we never actually used it. Let's pass the name of a key pair from a root template to the module and use it for our `aws_instance` resource:

```
module "mighty_trousers" {
  source = "./modules/application"
  vpc_id = "${aws_vpc.my_vpc.id}"
  subnet_id = "${aws_subnet.public.id}"
  name = "MightyTrousers"
  keypair = "${aws_key_pair.terraform.key_name}"
  environment = "${var.environment}"
  extra_sgs = ["${aws_security_group.default.id}"]
  extra_packages = "${lookup(var.extra_packages, "MightyTrousers")}"
  external_nameserver = "${var.external_nameserver}"
}
```

Add a new `variable` to the application module:

```
variable "keypair" {}
```

And use it inside the module:

```
resource "aws_instance" "app-server" {
  ami = "${data.aws_ami.app-ami.id}"
  instance_type = "${lookup(var.instance_type, var.environment)}"
  subnet_id = "${var.subnet_id}"
  vpc_security_group_ids = ["${concat(var.extra_sgs,
aws_security_group.allow_http.*.id)}"]
  user_data = "${data.template_file.user_data.rendered}"
  key_name = "${var.keypair}"
  tags {
    Name = "${var.name}"
  }
}
```

Changing a key pair requires instance recreation, but that's fine because we didn't have a production instance running - we don't have to bother with a safe replacement procedure yet. Just run `terraform apply` again and give it a minute to run.

> What we are doing now can be considered a **Test Drive Development**: we started with a failing test, and now we are slowly moving to make it green.

Connecting with Other Tools

After it's done, rerun the tests and see them go green:

```
$> inspec exec specs/base_spec.rb -t ssh://centos@$
  (terraform output mighty_trousers_public_ip) -i ~/.ssh/id_rsa
Target: ssh://centos@52.57.242.158:22
System Package
  wget should be installed
Test Summary: 1 successful, 0 failures, 0 skipped
```

This works well for testing a single server, but most likely, your infrastructure has more than one server. You have full flexibility on how to test them. The simplest option is to wrap both *Terraform* and *Inspec* into another shell script. We will take a look at some more sophisticated setups in a bit. What's important to memorize for now is that it is really easy to connect Terraform to external tools just using outputs. However, of course, it's only one of multiple ways of doing it. Another way is to use *provisioners*.

> Don't take it as a valid example of how to test a single server with Inspec. If you want to perform tests like this, Terraform is the wrong tool to spin up the server. Consider using Test Kitchen (discussed in Chapter 7, *Collaborative Infrastructure*).

Provisioners

Provisioners in Terraform are configuration blocks available for several resources that allow you to perform some actions after the resource has been created. It is mostly useful for servers, such as EC2 instances. Provisioners can be used to bootstrap the instance, to connect it to a cluster or to run tests, as we did manually in the previous section. There are the following four types of provisioners:

- local-exec
- remote-exec
- file
- chef

Each of them has its own applications and is useful for solving one issue or another. Let's take local-exec first and see how it can help in building inventory files for Ansible.

Provisioning with local-exec and Ansible

Ansible is one of the newest and hottest open source configuration management tools. It has become increasingly popular due to its ease of use. One of the main differences with Chef and Puppet is the lack of any agent installed on the machine to configure. The only requirement is that the machine has Python preinstalled, which is most often the case anyway.

Ansible is executed via SSH. You can run ad-hoc commands to execute trivial scripts on servers, as well as apply Ansible playbooks - definitions of server configuration written in YAML format, analogous to Chef cookbooks and Puppet modules. Ansible needs an inventory file to be able to run a playbook or ad-hoc commands. An inventory is just a text file with a hostname on each line and optional grouping of hosts by putting a group name in square brackets just preceding the hostnames in this group. Let's use Terraform to add an entry to the inventory file after the new EC2 instance is provisioned.

First, make sure you have Python and `pip` installed. Depending on the operating system, it could be either already installed or available for installation via a system package manager.

Once `pip` is available, installing Ansible is a single command away:

```
$> pip install ansible
```

Now let's add a provisioner to `./modules/application/application.tf`:

```
resource "aws_instance" "app-server" {
  ami = "${data.aws_ami.app-ami.id}"
  instance_type = "${lookup(var.instance_type, var.environment)}"
  subnet_id = "${var.subnet_id}"
  vpc_security_group_ids = ["${concat(var.extra_sgs,
aws_security_group.allow_http.*.id)}"]
  user_data = "${data.template_file.user_data.rendered}"
  key_name = "${var.keypair}"
  provisioner "local-exec" {
    command = "echo ${self.public_ip} >> inventory"
  }
  tags {
    Name = "${var.name}"
  }
}
```

Inside provisioners (and only inside provisioners) we can use a special keyword `self` to access attributes of a resource being provisioned. The command of provisioner is executed relative to the folder you are running Terraform from.

Connecting with Other Tools

Apply the template. Notice that provisioners will run only once, after resource creation. None of the updates will re-trigger provisioning, so if you had your stack created before, then destroy it and start creation again. Or use your knowledge about the `terraform taint` command to recreate only the EC2 instance.

After you have the public IP address in an inventory file, you can try running Ansible:

```
$> ansible all -i inventory -a "cat /etc/redhat-release" -u centos
35.156.10.103 | SUCCESS | rc=0 >>
CentOS Linux release 7.2.1511 (Core)
```

It might take a few minutes for AWS to upload the public key to the instance. Don't be surprised if it doesn't work on the first attempt.

Clearly, this implementation doesn't scale very well. Sooner or later we will have multiple machines having different roles: application servers, database servers, and so on. One option would be to create an inventory file beforehand with host groups predefined inside, as follows:

```
[app-server]
[db-server]
```

Then, we could extend the `local-exec` provisioner to be a little bit smarter:

```
provisioner "local-exec" {
  command = "sed -i '/\\[app-server\\]/a ${self.public_ip}' inventory"
}
```

With some *sed* magic, we will add the application server to the `[app-server]` host group. This will allow us to write more granular Ansible code. Note double slashes: we need to escape brackets both for *sed* and for Terraform.

The process of creating and provisioning the complete infrastructure could look as follows:

- Run the Terraform template to create servers and populate the inventory file
- Run the Ansible playbook to configure all instances in all groups

This approach has some flaws though. For example, it doesn't handle deleted servers: if the instance is gone from the Terraform template, it will still exist in the inventory file generated previously, leading to failed Ansible runs. Neither do we have any indicator of SSH being ready: if we stay with this approach, we have to basically guess if an instance is ready to be SSHed to. Not good!

It would be nice if Terraform had built-in Ansible support, but it's not the case yet. However, there is a small utility named `terraform-inventory` that generates a dynamic Ansible inventory from the Terraform state file. It is available for download on GitHub at https://github.com/adammck/terraform-inventory. You need to use it after running Terraform, as follows:

```
$> ansible all -i ~/bin/terraform-inventory -a "cat /etc/redhat-release" -u centos
```

> Besides static text file inventories, Ansible has **dynamic inventories**, meaning that you can pass a script that generates an inventory on the fly. That's why the command mentioned previously works.

It's important to understand that Terraform is a tool that focuses on doing exactly one job, and quite often, you will need to add some extra tools that either support Terraform or extend its area of usage. Luckily, there are external programs that can make life with Terraform a little bit easier, like the Terraform inventory we just saw. We will cover a few other tools a bit later.

The `local-exec` provisioner is a powerful way to trigger some scripts from the machine that is running Terraform commands. Earlier, we used outputs to pass an IP address to Inspec. With `local-exec`, we can remove the manual step of running the `inspec` command: just put this command inside the provisioner and pass the IP by interpolating the `aws_instance` attribute. This sounds like a great exercise for you! After you are done with it, proceed further.

Although there is no built-in Ansible support, there is Chef support that works out-of-the-box. Let's take a quick look at it.

Provisioning with Chef

Chef is a much older, mature solution to configure management. Unlike Ansible, it does require an installation of an agent on each server, named **chef-client**. Also, unlike Ansible, it has a **Chef server** that each client pulls configuration from. We will not install the complete Chef server, because doing so could take up the rest of the chapter. If you know and use Chef, then keep reading. If you don't, skip to the next section.

There are two places where Chef APIs are used in Terraform:

- A Chef provisioner
- A Chef provider

A Chef provisioner allows you to specify all the details to connect to a Chef server, an initial set of attributes, and the run list. Once an instance is created, Terraform will SSH into it, install **chef-client,** and try to register it with Chef server using the configuration you provided in your template:

```
provisioner "chef"  {
    run_list = ["cookbook::recipe"]
    node_name = "app-server-1"
    server_url = "https://chef.internal/organizations/my_company"
    recreate_client = true
    user_name = "packt"
    user_key = "${file("packt.pem")}"
}
```

The `recreate_client` option is important: without it, you can't reregister the server if it had to be recreated. There are many more parameters you can configure for a Chef provisioner. For full reference, you should consult the Terraform documentation.

The other part, Chef provider, allows you to create various entities on a Chef server. You could create a node with a Chef provider as well, but it's not recommended because it doesn't actually install chef-client anywhere. You could use the provider to store and update all your **Chef roles** as code:

```
resource "chef_role" "app-server" {
  name = "app-server"
  run_list = ["recipe[nginx]"]
}
```

There are two things to consider before using Terraform with Chef though:

- First, Chef itself already has the capabilities to store all of its resources as code, in a dedicated Chef repository. Normally, all roles, data bags, and so on are already stored in a version control system in a plan JSON format, and using Terraform for this purpose has little to no benefit.

- Second, if you use Chef heavily, then you might not need Terraform at all. Chef already has the Chef provisioning component that solves exactly the same problem as Terraform: allows you to define your infrastructure in a single template. It has a few extra benefits, like being platform agnostic for base resources: servers, networks, and others. It has downsides as well: it is not as actively developed as Terraform (and looks more and more like a deprecated project) and the list of supported providers is not that long. But if you use AWS and Chef, then bringing Terraform into the picture might not be the best decision to make.

In order for Terraform to use the Chef provisioner, it has to have SSH access to the server. This SSH access doesn't have to be used only to set up Chef though. That brings us to the `remote-exec` provisioner.

Provisioning with remote-exec and Puppet

Each provisioner that needs to connect to the instance has a connection block defined. This block is responsible for either SSH or WinRM configuration so that Terraform knows how, with which user, password (or key) to connect to the server. You can execute any scripts on the target server via this connection with the help of the `remote-exec` provisioner.

There is a built-in Chef provisioner, and it's rather easy to use Ansible (because it doesn't need anything installed on the target system), but what about Puppet? It works very similarly to Chef, with the same server-client model, and it requires Puppet agents to be installed. Let's do it with `remote-exec`.

> We could put its installation into the `cloud-init` script, but then we wouldn't be able to use it for the `remote-exec` demonstration.

First, prepare `modules/application/application.tf` for `remote-exec`: remove any `local-exec` and Chef provisioners you've added before.

Then, let's configure a connection block. The default username to SSH into CentOS 7 AMI is `"centos"`, and we need to specify it in the template:

```
provisioner "remote-exec" {
  connection {
    user = "centos"
  }
}
```

Connecting with Other Tools

This should be enough to get going, but if you are using a false private key, then you need to specify it in the same block:

```
provisioner "remote-exec" {
  connection {
    user = "centos"
    private_key = "${file("/home/johndoe/.ssh/my_private_key.pem")}"
  }
}
```

> You could also use an SSH-agent with the Boolean `agent` parameter. In a team, you don't want to hardcode the path to your private key; this path is different for each of your colleagues. Using SSH-agent solves this problem.

Sometimes, your servers are not publicly available via SSH. Your database server, for example, is probably inside a private subnet, and in order to access it, you need to use a so-called **bastion host**. Terraform has got you covered here as well, with bastion configuration options:

```
connection {
  user = "centos"
  agent = true
  bastion_host = "my_bastion.com"
  bastion_user = "centos"
  bastion_private_key = "${file("/home/johndoe/.ssh/bastion_key.pem")}"
}
```

There is the same wide set of configuration options for WinRM connections, although bastion host can be configured only for SSH connections.

There are three ways to provide a script: inline in the template, by specifying a path to the script, or by specifying the whole array of paths to different scripts that will be executed in the order you provide them. Let's keep it simple and provide the script inline first:

```
provisioner "remote-exec" {
  connection {
    user = "centos"
  }
  inline = [
    "sudo rpm -ivh http://yum.puppetlabs.com/puppetlabs-release-el-7.noarch.rpm",
    "sudo yum install puppet -y"
  ]
}
```

Connecting with Other Tools

This will install the Puppet `yum` repository and Puppet itself. It's a bit silly to install Puppet and not to use it though. We need to configure something with it.

Although scalable secure Puppet environments often assume **Puppet master** is in place, it's easy to use Puppet in masterless mode as well. To do so, we can use the `puppet apply` command that requires a manifest file (configuration description written in Puppet language). But there is no manifest file on the server! We need to put it there somehow. File provisioner will help us with that.

Uploading files with a file provisioner

A file provisioner simply uploads a file to the server. It's a perfect way to upload configuration files, certificates, and so on. Create a new file named `setup.pp` in the `./modules/application/` folder with the following content:

```
host { 'repository':
  ip => '10.24.45.127',
}
```

Puppet's `host` resource will add a host entry on the machine. Normally, we should not hardcode host entries on the machine. However, sometimes, it doesn't have access to the DNS server yet, but it already needs to install some packages from an internal repository. That's the use case our manifest will cover. We just need to upload it.

Because we will end up with two different provisioners: `file` and `remote-exec`, we should move connection block outside the `remote-exec` provisioner and define it on a resource level. The file provisioner is simple: we only need to specify the source file and destination:

```
resource "aws_instance" "app-server" {
  ami = "${data.aws_ami.app-ami.id}"
  instance_type = "${lookup(var.instance_type, var.environment)}"
  subnet_id = "${var.subnet_id}"
  vpc_security_group_ids = ["${concat(var.extra_sgs,
aws_security_group.allow_http.*.id)}"]
  user_data = "${data.template_file.user_data.rendered}"
  key_name = "${var.keypair}"
  connection {
    user = "centos"
  }
  provisioner "file" {
    source = "${path.module}/setup.pp"
    destination = "/tmp/setup.pp"
  }
```

```
    provisioner "remote-exec" {
      inline = [
        "sudo rpm -ivh
http://yum.puppetlabs.com/puppetlabs-release-el-7.noarch.rpm",
        "sudo yum install puppet -y",
        "sudo puppet apply /tmp/setup.pp"
      ]
    }
    tags {
      Name = "${var.name}"
    }
  }
```

Destroy the template or taint the `aws_instance` resource and apply it again to rerun provisioners. Terraform will output everything from scripts to the console, so you should see something like the following:

```
module.mighty_trousers.aws_instance.app-server (remote-exec): Complete!
module.mighty_trousers.aws_instance.app-server (remote-exec):
Notice: Compiled catalog for ip-10-0-1-127.eu-central-1.compute.internal
in environment production in 0.07 seconds
module.mighty_trousers.aws_instance.app-server (remote-exec): Notice:
/Stage[main]/Main/Host[repository]/ensure: created
module.mighty_trousers.aws_instance.app-server (remote-exec):
Notice: Finished catalog run in 0.02 seconds
```

Even without the built-in support for Puppet, it appears to be relatively simple to use it with Terraform. Perhaps a bit more complicated in a server-client setup (you need to handle node registration properly), but still nothing too complicated. That's the flexibility `remote-exec` brings.

One question that could be raised is: why would I use provisioners instead of `cloud-init`? This is a valid question, and there is exactly one big reason to use provisioners: dependency management inside Terraform. If you use `cloud-init`, then there is no way to order the creation of different resources inside the Terraform template, simply because Terraform has no idea when cloud-init has finished its job. And that's a problem if you have some kind of master that should exist before every slave node is provisioned, because a slave needs a master to exist. With provisioners, it's not a problem: the resource is not considered as created till provisioning is finished. This means that if resource A depends on resource B, Terraform won't start creating it till all provisioners of resource B are finished.

So far, all provisioners you have learned are meant to be used with one resource, and all of them are impossible to rerun without recreating the resource it provisions. In this situation, `null_resource` is our friend.

> While this book is about Terraform, you should always know your options. Similar to Chef, Puppet has built-in ways to do the same job as Terraform: to describe the infrastructure in a single template. In the case of Puppet, it has its own powerful language that allows Puppet modules such as `puppetlabs-aws` (https://github.com/puppetlabs/puppetlabs-aws) to describe all of your cloud resources in an idempotent way. Again, if you are a heavy Puppet user, consider the features it has before bringing extra tools such as Terraform into your company.

Reprovisioning machines with null_resource

`null_resource` doesn't create anything. It's a container for provisioners. Because it is not directly connected to any piece of the infrastructure, it's not a big deal to destroy it in order to retrigger provisioners it has defined on.

There are two types of provisioning we are doing right now with Puppet: the one-time Puppet installation and Puppet run, which should be retriggered if the manifest changes-- imagine that the repository IP changed and somehow we still don't have a proper DNS server in place.

> If you have Puppet master, all of it makes zero sense: modules and manifests are stored on the master, and the Puppet agent runs as a system service and applies manifests automatically every N minutes. On the contrary, this approach can be very handy if you decide to go for a masterless setup, because in that case, you have a whole new set of problems of how to distribute your Puppet code to all the servers you have.

Slim down the provisioners of the `aws_instance` resource to look like following:

```
connection {
  user = "centos"
}
provisioner "remote-exec" {
  inline = [
    "sudo rpm -ivh http://yum.puppetlabs.com/puppetlabs-release-el-7.noarch.rpm",
    "sudo yum install puppet -y",
  ]
}
```

Now, let's define `null_resource` right after `aws_instance`. Note the `triggers` block: it allows you to specify when exactly to recreate `null_resource`. In this case, it will be *recreated* if the instance was recreated, thus rerunning the provisioning automatically:

```
resource "null_resource" "app_server_provisioner" {
  triggers {
    server_id = "${aws_instance.app-server.id}"
  }
  connection {
    user = "centos"
    host = "${aws_instance.app-server.public_ip}"
  }
  provisioner "file" {
    source = "${path.module}/setup.pp"
    destination = "/tmp/setup.pp"
  }
  provisioner "remote-exec" {
    inline = [
      "sudo puppet apply /tmp/setup.pp"
    ]
  }
}
```

This `null_resource` would run only after the EC2 instance was provisioned because it depends on it. It will rerun (meaning *provisioners will rerun*) if the instance is changed. And you can force the run of provisioners with our old friend `taint` command:

```
$> terraform taint –module mighty_trousers
null_resource.app_server_provisioner
```

Such reprovisioning is only one of many ways you can use `null_resource`. It's a simple tool, but it gives you the ability to create really complex provisioning scenarios, with multiple connections to different servers, local and remote scripts, and data pulled from different sources. With a tool such as bootstrapping clusters, building complex Ansible inventories and triggering test pipelines becomes a piece of cake.

You have now learned everything there that is there to learn about Terraform provisioners. As we've seen, it's rather easy to invoke any other tool via the usage or combination of `remote-exec`, `local-exec`, and `null_resource`. But it's not always that convenient to use them, especially if there is a better alternative in the form of third-party plugins.

Using third-party plugins

Regardless of how convenient it is to connect Terraform with other external tools, such as configuration management systems, one would always prefer a built-in, native solution. An example is, as discussed previously, the Chef provisioner: while it's possible to do exactly the same with `remote-exec`, it's much faster to use a special provisioner written just for this purpose. Unfortunately, while the list of supported providers is long, some of the technologies or services you need will be missing.

Luckily, Terraform has a plugin-based architecture, and it's trivial to extend it with custom providers and provisioners. Plugins are written in the Go programming language, and if you want to write your own, you need to have at least basic knowledge of it.

There are plugins available on GitHub that you could use. Ideally, developers should contribute these providers and provisioners to the Terraform core. Sometimes, though, it's not possible: it takes time to create and test a fully functional provider or provisioner and, sometimes, these third-party plugins, while being ready to use, are not yet accepted by Terraform core team.

This should not stop you from using them though. You just have to be careful, and keep in mind that they are more likely to have bugs than providers that are already part of the Terraform.

If you have been following the latest trends in the operations world, then you might have heard about Kubernetes. In essence, it's an orchestration tool for containers which gives you automated deployment, scaling, and management of containers, regardless of which containers tool you use, be it Docker, rkt, or something else. Kubernetes has many components and entities to manage, such as pods (groups of containers) and services. It's a perfect candidate to be managed by Terraform. And because it's such a complex, big provider it takes a while to get it right. As a result, at the moment, it is still not part of Terraform, but you can still use it as a plugin.

> **The Terraform-provider-kubernetes** source code is stored at GitHub: https://github.com/maxmanuylov/terraform-provider-kubernetes. To get the latest version running, you would have to compile it yourself, installing Go beforehand. There are already-compiled and ready-to-use releases though, also available at GitHub: https://github.com/maxmanuylov/terraform-provider-kubernetes/releases.

In order to install a plugin, you first need to download it and make it available as part of your PATH environment variable:

```
$> wget https://github.com/maxmanuylov/terraform-provider-kubernetes/releases/download/v1.0-beta.3/terraform-provider-kubernetes-v1.0-beta.3-linux.tar.gz
$> tar -xzf terraform-provider-kubernetes-v1.0-beta.3-linux.tar.gz
```

Then, you need to activate it by adding it to the `~/.terraformrc` file, as follows:

```
providers {
    kubernetes = "/path/to/terraform-provider-kubernetes"
}
```

In this case, `kubernetes` is a prefix for all resources. If you want to have some fun, you can name it `borg` and then all resources will have to prefixed with `borg` instead of `kubernetes`. But then, it's rather confusing for your team.

> Borg is the name of the internal Google orchestration system. Kubernetes design is based on Borg and is an improved version of it.

That's everything there is to do to make the plugin available. You can use all Kubernetes resources inside your template now, as follows:

```
resource "kubernetes_resource" "mypod" {
  cluster = "${kubernetes_cluster.main.cluster}"
  collection = "pods"
  name = "mypod"
  content = "${file("mypod.yaml")}"
}
```

Another useful third-party plugin is `terraform-provisioner-ansible` that, you guessed right, adds Ansible support to Terraform. The source code of this plugin is available on GitHub: https://github.com/jonmorehouse/terraform-provisioner-ansible. It appears to be nonfunctional with the latest Terraform releases though. As with every other third-party plugin, you should use it at your own risk.

Summary

In this chapter, you learned a lot of new technologies, which, can be combined with Terraform to perfect your infrastructure as code setup. We practiced every type of provisioner Terraform has, specifically, the following:

- Executed tests with Inspec and Terraform outputs
- Generated inventory files for Ansible with `local-exec`
- Created new Chef nodes with the Chef provisioner
- Installed the Puppet agent with `remote-exec` and uploaded Puppet manifests with a file provisioner
- Made reusable provisioning with `null_resource`

We also took a look at a few third-party plugins, which are, unfortunately, of low quality, often unsupported, and have bugs. You should normally use both built-in providers and provisioners, or implement something with existing provisioners.

In the next chapter, we will go to the next level of managing infrastructure with Terraform. You will actually learn how to continuously manage an existing infrastructure. We will see what Terraform provides in terms of scaling infrastructure, and how to perform complex update scenarios.

6
Scaling and Updating Infrastructure

Honestly, you already know almost everything about Terraform now. Creating networks in the Cloud? Easy. Starting a new virtual server and provisioning it with your favorite configuration management tool? Isn't it a piece of cake?! You know how to write a beautiful template, refactor it into modules, and configure it with the many ways that there are to configure a template.

Perhaps you even moved your whole infrastructure to Terraform. But then you realize that creating infrastructure with Terraform is just the beginning; that is, your infrastructure is there to stay, and it needs to be updated continuously as your business requirements change.

There are many challenges in managing the resources you have. We need to figure out how to perform changes without interrupting the service. We will take a look at the following and some other topics in this chapter:

- The means of scaling the service up and down with Terraform
- Performing an in-place upgrade of a server and how to do rolling updates
- How to perform blue-green deployments
- How to scale automatically with the Auto Scaling groups of AWS
- What is immutable infrastructure is and how the tool named Packer helps to achieve that

Before proceeding with this chapter, destroy all your previously created resources with the `terraform destroy` command. We are starting from a clean state again.

Counting servers

So far, we have created only one EC2 instance for the web application `MightyTrousers`. As the popularity of the app increases, a single server can't handle the load properly anymore. We could scale vertically by increasing the instance size, but it would still leave us with a single server that handles all the critical traffic. In a cloud world, you should assume that absolutely every machine you have can be gone at any moment. You should be prepared for worst case scenarios: a **distributed denial-of-service (DDoS)** attack putting your cluster on its knees, an earthquake destroying the whole data center, an internal AWS outage, and many others.

Thus, not only as a way to scale the infrastructure, but also to make the application highly available, we should increase the number of instances we have. And it's not only about the number of them, but also the location of each of them: keeping 20 instances in a single place still puts you in a situation where the outage of one data center puts you out of business; while 10 instances each in two data centers in two different geographical locations will keep your software running even in the event of a worst case scenario for one of data centers.

Terraform, being a tool based on declarative DSL, doesn't have loops as part of its language. If we were to do it in a regular programming language, let's say Ruby, we would write something like the following:

```
5.times do
   create ec2_instnace
end
```

Chef combines both declarative and imperative approaches, which would be a reasonable (though, not on every occasion) thing to do. However, in Terraform, we don't and can't tell the tool what to do. We tell Terraform what should exist as part of our infrastructure, and the specifics of creation are handled by the tool itself. That's why, instead of iterating over the same resource, Terraform gives as an extra property, responsible for defining how many resources of the same kind should exist. It's named `count`.

Using it is simple: for every resource that needs to be created more than once, you just specify the `count` parameter to be equal to the number you desire:

```
resource "aws_instance" "my-app" {
   ...
   count = 5
}
```

Scaling and Updating Infrastructure

One problem with `count` is that it cannot be used with modules. In our case, it's not really a big problem though; we want to multiply the number of instances created in the module, while keeping only one security group for all of them. Still, as we don't want to hardcode any values, we need a way to pass the required number of instances to the module.

As we are already well familiar with variables, let's just add one more to the application module in the `modules/application/variables.tf` file:

```
...
variable "instance_count" { default = 0 }
```

Let's use it straight away:

```
resource "aws_instance" "app-server" {
  ami = "${data.aws_ami.app-ami.id}"
  instance_type = "${lookup(var.instance_type, var.environment)}"
  subnet_id = "${var.subnet_id}"
  vpc_security_group_ids = ["${concat(var.extra_sgs,
aws_security_group.allow_http.*.id)}"]
  user_data = "${data.template_file.user_data.rendered}"
  key_name = "${var.keypair}"
  connection {
    user = "centos"
  }
  provisioner "remote-exec" {
    inline = [
      "sudo rpm -ivh http://yum.puppetlabs.com/puppetlabs-release-el-7.noarch.rpm",
      "sudo yum install puppet -y",
    ]
  }
  tags {
    Name = "${var.name}"
  }
  count = "${var.instance_count}"
}
```

Now, pass the variable to the module:

```
module "mighty_trousers" {
  source = "./modules/application"
  ...
  instance_count = 2
}
```

[109]

Scaling and Updating Infrastructure

We can try to apply our template now, but trust me, it won't be a success:

```
$> terraform plan
Refreshing Terraform state in-memory prior to plan...
The refreshed state will be used to calculate this plan, but
will not be persisted to local or remote state storage.
module.mighty_trousers.data.template_file.user_data: Refreshing
state...
module.mighty_trousers.data.aws_ami.app-ami: Refreshing state...
Error running plan: 1 error(s) occurred:
* Resource 'aws_instance.app-server' does not have attribute 'id'
for variable
'aws_instance.app-server.id'
```

The problem here is that we are using the `aws_instance` resource in the `null_provisioner`, defined in the previous chapter:

```
resource "null_resource" "app_server_provisioner" {
  # ....
  connection {
    user = "centos"
    host = "${aws_instance.app-server.public_ip}"
  }
}
```

We configured this provisioner when we had only one EC2 instance, but now, as Terraform creates two of them, it's not valid anymore. It's not the only occurrence of this mistake: the `public_ip` output also assumes that there is just one instance.

There are two ways to fix it:

- Take only the first instance created
- Get values from all instances

It actually won't fix `null_resource` for us, so just for the sake of demonstration, comment it out. We will fix it in a bit.

> To comment out, put a hash sign (#) in front of the line.

Scaling and Updating Infrastructure

Now, if we want to access one particular instance from the list, we can reference it as follows: `aws_instance.app-server.$NUMBER.public_ip`. Try it out:

```
output "public_ip" {
  value = "${aws_instance.app-server.0.public_ip}"
}
```

The Terraform plan is now successfully completed. But, well, that's kind of useless, isn't it? We need all addresses to be returned from the module. That's where the `join()` function becomes handy: it allows you to build a single string from the values of all elements in a list. The following example speaks for itself:

```
output "public_ip" {
  value = "${join(",", aws_instance.app-server.*.public_ip)}"
}
```

If you were to try to apply the template like this is, you would get an almost satisfying result:

```
Outputs:
mighty_trousers_public_ip = 35.156.29.192,35.156.32.127
```

This output is good only if it returns the IPs of servers that were properly provisioned, so let's get back to fixing the `null_provisioner`. This is how it should look now, before it works with multiple instances:

```
resource "null_resource" "app_server_provisioner" {
  triggers {
    server_id = "${aws_instance.app-server.id}"
  }
  connection {
    user = "centos"
    host = "${aws_instance.app-server.public_ip}"
  }

  provisioner "file" {
    source = "${path.module}/setup.pp"
    destination = "/tmp/setup.pp"
  }

  provisioner "remote-exec" {
    inline = [
      "sudo puppet apply /tmp/setup.pp"
    ]
  }
}
```

Scaling and Updating Infrastructure

The first thing to fix here is the `triggers` block. It needs to take all instances into consideration, and we can do so with the same `join()` function:

```
triggers {
  server_id = "${join(",", aws_instance.app-server.*.id)}"
}
```

This will, of course, fix the problem with retriggering the provisioner. But it still provisions only one instance, as you can see in the following line:

```
host = "${aws_instance.app-server.public_ip}"
```

The problem becomes more complicated: we can't go further with just a single provisioner for multiple instances, and this *1-n* relationship simply won't work:

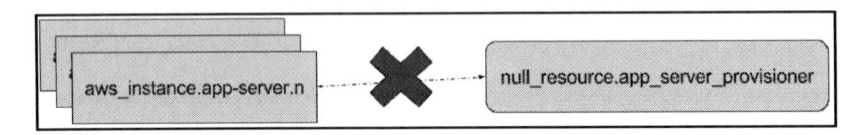

Rather, what we need is something like the following:

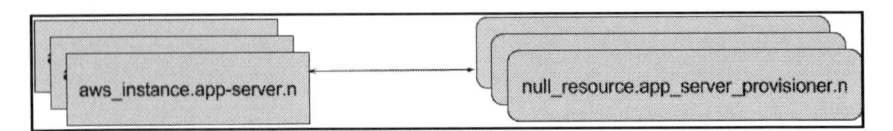

This means that, first of all, we need to add the `count` parameter to `null_resource` as well. It would be the same `instance_count` variable used for the `aws_instance` resource. The trick here is that, right inside resource configuration, you can access the index of the particular instance of this resource via the `${count.index}` variable, which, combined with the `element()` function, allows us to query attributes on the other list of the same size--the list of instances. With this change, the complete `null_resource` block should look as follows (notice the highlighted connection block):

```
resource "null_resource" "app_server_provisioner" {
  triggers {
    server_id = "${join(",", aws_instance.app-server.*.id)}"
  }
  connection {   user = "centos"   host = "${element(aws_instance.app-server.*.public_ip,
                 count.index)}"   }
  provisioner "file" {
    source = "${path.module}/setup.pp"
    destination = "/tmp/setup.pp"
```

```
  }
  provisioner "remote-exec" {
    inline = [
      "sudo puppet apply /tmp/setup.pp"
    ]
  }
  count = "${var.instance_count}"
}
```

This pattern can be seen in Terraform templates quite often: binding two or more groups of resources with lookups like this. We don't have the need to do so here, but it is also common to do the same for the `user_data` attribute and the `template_file` data resource combination, if user data needs an index as a variable.

With this new fancy count-involved configuration, you might be tempted to finally apply the template. Go ahead and do so. You will notice a few things. For example, the log output for counted resource looks as follows:

```
module.mighty_trousers.null_resource.app_server_provisioner.0
```

It looks the same in the `state` file as well:

```
"null_resource.app_server_provisioner.0": {
#  ...
```

If you examine the body of one of the `null_resource` in the `state` file, you will also note this part:

```
"attributes": {
  "id": "9043342603318320402",
  "triggers.%": "1",
  "triggers.server_id": "i-85e9d839,i-86e9d83a"
},
```

And there is a bug right here for you to fix: every provisioner for every instance will be retriggered, even if only one of the instances changes. Our triggers are wrong, and it's up to you to fix it with the `element()` function.

While it's nice to have two instances--we can handle twice as much traffic now--we are still far away from being **highly available (HA)**.

Bringing in high availability

With AWS, going HA can be as simple as putting instances into different subnets assigned to different availability zones. An availability zone is an isolated location within one AWS region, and you can look at it as a separate data center.

We are passing subnet ID as a variable to the application module, and we are passing exactly one subnet ID. This needs to be changed, that is, we will update the `subnet_id` variable to be the list of two elements. Then, depending on the index of an `aws_instance` resource, we will assign either the first or the second subnet to it.

First of all, replace the `subnet_id` variable with the `subnets` variable and specify the type as `list` to avoid anything else being passed to the module:

```
variable "subnets"    { type = "list "}
```

> If you set the default value of `variable` to be `[]`, then Terraform will understand that this variable is a list.

In root template, we need to change the `subnet_cidr` variable to make it availability zone aware and to extend it to support four subnets:

```
variable "subnet_cidrs" {
  description = "CIDR blocks for public and private subnets"
  default = {
    "eu-central-1a-public" = "10.0.1.0/24",
    "eu-central-1a-private" = "10.0.2.0/24",
    "eu-central-1b-public" = "10.0.3.0/24",
    "eu-central-1b-private" = "10.0.4.0/24"
  }
}
```

Terraform doesn't support nested maps as of version 0.8.1, so we have to make this variable a bit uglier than it should be in a perfect world. Use this new variable inside `template.tf` (similar code for a private subnet is omitted):

```
resource "aws_subnet" "public-1" {
  vpc_id = "${aws_vpc.my_vpc.id}"
  availability_zone = "eu-central-1a"
  cidr_block = "${lookup(var.subnet_cidrs, "eu-central-1a-public")}"
  map_public_ip_on_launch = true
}
resource "aws_subnet" "public-2" {
  vpc_id = "${aws_vpc.my_vpc.id}"
```

```
    availability_zone = "eu-central-1b"
    cidr_block = "${lookup(var.subnet_cidrs, "eu-central-1b-public")}"
    map_public_ip_on_launch = true
}
```

Perhaps when you see this slightly repetitive code, you will want to refactor it to be a single `aws_subnet` resource with a count of 2. It's not forbidden to do so, of course, but it would be a rather hard-to-digest piece of code. When you choose between a minor duplication and adding more complexity, choose minor duplication. It is a harder choice when you are dealing with it in the programming world, but don't be fooled: writing Terraform templates is not real programming, it's more similar to writing configuration files.

It's been a long period of time during which Terraform hasn't supported passing lists and maps as variables to modules. These harsh times are gone and, starting from version 0.7, you can do it. So, let's do it and pass a subnets list to the application module!

```
module "mighty_trousers" {
  source = "./modules/application"
  vpc_id = "${aws_vpc.my_vpc.id}"
  subnets = ["${aws_subnet.public-1.id}", "${aws_subnet.public-2.id}"]
  name = "MightyTrousers"
  keypair = "${aws_key_pair.terraform.key_name}"
  environment = "${var.environment}"
  extra_sgs = ["${aws_security_group.default.id}"]
  extra_packages = "${lookup(var.extra_packages, "MightyTrousers")}"
  external_nameserver = "${var.external_nameserver}"
  instance_count = 2
}
```

The only thing left is to use these subnets inside `aws_instance`. We will need the `element()` function again, as well as the modulo math operation: we will use the first subnet for even instances and the second one for odd instances:

```
resource "aws_instance" "app-server" {
  ami = "${data.aws_ami.app-ami.id}"
  instance_type = "${lookup(var.instance_type, var.environment)}"
  subnet_id = "${element(var.subnets, count.index % 2)}"
}
```

With this code, we can easily scale our application to any number of instances, and they will be evenly distributed among availability zones. Nice and easy. High availability achieved. Well, almost. We need to put a load balancer in front of these application servers first.

Load balancing and simulating conditionals

If we were not using AWS in this book, or if we wanted to go the more complicated (but certainly more flexible) way, we would use our very own load balancer. But we won't, because we can simply take the **Elastic Load Balancer (ELB)** service of AWS and put application servers behind it.

This means we will add yet another resource to the application module. Add the following configuration right after the `null_resource` provisioners:

```
resource "aws_elb" "load-balancer" {
  name = "application-load-balancer"
  subnets = ["${var.subnets}"]
  security_groups = "${aws_security_group.allow_http.id}"]

  listener {
    instance_port = 80
    instance_protocol = "http"
    lb_port = 80
    lb_protocol = "http"
  }

  health_check {
    healthy_threshold = 2
    unhealthy_threshold = 2
    timeout = 3
    target = "TCP:80"
    interval = 30
  }

  instances = ["${aws_instance.app-server.*.id}"]
}
```

This ELB is configured for the `HTTP` port, and it has a health check that will verify that an instance is actually listening on this port. It is configured to balance the list of application servers we have and to work in two subnets, already passed via a variable.

Scaling and Updating Infrastructure

With ELB in place, we probably want to output its DNS name instead of the list of public IP addresses of instances: also, because now we don't have to expose them to the internet. Remove the `public_ip` output and add a new one instead:

```
output "app_address" {
  value = "${aws_elb.load-balancer.dns_name}"
}
```

Do this to the root template as well:

```
output "mighty_trousers_app_address" {
  value = "${module.mighty_trousers.app_address}"
}
```

We cannot verify that everything works as expected for one simple reason: we have never installed anything that listens on port 80 on any of our machines. Let's modify our Puppet manifest to install and start Apache and then reprovision instances via `null_resource`!

Make the contents of `setup.pp` look as follows:

```
package { 'httpd':
  ensure => installed
}
service { 'httpd':
  ensure  => running,
  require => [
    Package['httpd'],
  ],
}
```

This might not be the most sophisticated Apache Puppet setup you've seen, but it's enough to see a default Apache static page being served by an instance.

In order to trigger provisioning, we need to use our old friend `terraform taint` command. Previously, we've used it only with a single resource. It's not different with a group of resources, but you just need to provide an index. Terraform doesn't allow the use of wildcards in `taint`, which is a shame, because we have to run the `taint` command twice because of that:

```
$>terraform taint -module mighty_trousers
null_resource.app_server_provisioner.0
```

Run the `Terraform apply` command to get the web server running! As you have configured an output to get the hostname of ELB, copy it to your browser. You should see the following page in the end:

Let's recap what we did: we scaled up our application by adding one more instance. We then made it highly available by splitting instances into two different subnets. We have put them behind a load balancer. More than that, we configured these instances with Puppet without having to destroy anything! Apparently, we are getting very skilled at making our infrastructure more mature and we are already capable of performing some upgrades by combing Terraform with a configuration management tool.

But there is a catch: what if we don't need ELB just yet? What if it's just a development or staging environment that needs only one EC2 instance? Putting the single instance behind a load balancer would be a silly and wasteful move! We need to create a load balancer only if there is more than one instance.

Since Terraform 0.8, there is a conditionals support in Terraform DSL, but only inside interpolations. But there is still a trick to make the creation of resources conditional. The trick is quite trivial, actually. We just need to specify the `count` attribute on a load balancer. Don't worry; we won't create multiple load balancers.

In fact, we will create either 1 or 0 load balancers. Terraform allows `count` to equal 0, meaning that no resource creation is needed. So, if we want to skip the creation of ELB, we should set count to 0 in case only one instance was requested.

```
resource "aws_elb" "load-balancer" {
  name = "application-load-balancer"
  # ...
  instances = ["${aws_instance.app-server.*.id}"]
  count = "${var.instance_count > 1 ? 1 : 0}"
}
```

If you are stuck with the previous 0.8 version, then there is still a way to achieve the same result.

We only need to do some simple string matching, with the help of the `replace()` function and two tiny regular expressions:

```
resource "aws_elb" "load-balancer" {
  name = "application-load-balancer"
  # ...
  instances = ["${aws_instance.app-server.*.id}"]
  count = "${replace(replace(var.instance_count, "/^[1]{1}$/", "0"), "/^[1-9][0-9]*/", "1")}"
}
```

With this code, if the `instance_count` is "1", the number of ELBs to create will be 0. If it's anything other than 1, it will be 1. Verify it yourself by changing the `instance_count` variable to different values. Note that it won't work with an `instance_count` that equals 0 itself, but you can't avoid shooting yourself in the foot all the time.

Perhaps after seeing this count-based implementation of the simple `if` statement, you are horrified or even disgusted by Terraform. It's a valid reaction, but look at it from another angle: we managed to keep it as declarative as it gets. This ugly double `replace()` line allows you to determine the need to create ELB automatically, without additional variables.

In this case, adding another variable could also be a reasonable choice. You could simply create a variable named `has_lb` and use it as a simple indicator of whether you need ELB or not. And that's the correct approach if you need to do any kind of conditional creation with Terraform. You must agree, though, that usage of regular expressions and chains of function invocations, as we did earlier, makes you feel more proud of yourself.

Triggering Puppet runs is all nice and easy. If you really want to keep your infrastructure toolset as *spartan* as possible, you could even try to go further with only this approach. In reality, though, provisioning and reprovisioning machines only with Terraform is unlikely to be a solid automation foundation. It's not what Terraform was made for, and you will be much better off if you leave the configuration management part to a tool built for this, instead of making a shaky integration with Terraform.

What Terraform is better at, though, is performing upgrades of a complete server with a new one. But in order for Terraform to be able to do it, you need to follow a few additional steps. Let's talk about them and about performing rolling updates with Terraform. But, even before that, let's learn what immutable infrastructure is.

Immutable infrastructure

When we had bare metal servers, it took a bit of time to provision them. Even today, if you want to get new hardware, it can take days to get it connected and running. Needless to say that you would want to keep them running as long as possible, given the cost of replacement or adding a new one. Then, as automation is a must, instead of configuring these bare metal servers by hand, a set of configuration management tools appeared.

Even with these tools, though, servers are prone to configuration drift; they can diverge a lot from one another and people can still go via SSH and perform changes not captured in infrastructure code.

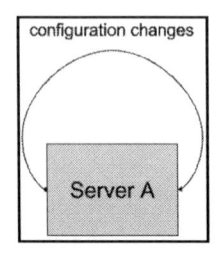

Don't get me wrong: configuration management is still a must. But the context changed a bit after virtualization was hugely adopted in the form of cloud providers. The time required to create a server was cut down to a few minutes, instead of hours and days. More importantly, the time required to recreate a server is also really low, compared with the bare metal world. So, why bother with keeping the existing machine updated if you could just destroy it and create a new one from scratch? That's the basis of a so-called **immutable Infrastructure**.

Scaling and Updating Infrastructure

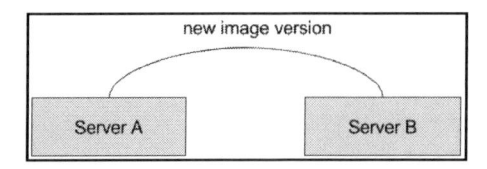

What does it give to operators?

- **Little to no configuration drift**: Your server is created once and is never updated, so you can just take a look at the base image to tell what is (most likely) the state of it.
- **Predictable and simple updates**: Each change to the configuration is captured and versioned in source control. It is then tested with tools such as Inspec and Test Kitchen. Only then, is it rolled out to environments, one at a time.

Immutable infrastructure goes hand in hand with functional programming principles: functional programming languages provide immutable data structures, just like your servers are immutable once they are created.

Netflix is perhaps the brightest example of the adoption of this approach. As they are one of the biggest AWS EC2 users, they run all of their workloads in the cloud on virtual servers. Their processes are well covered in multiple blog posts in the Netflix technology blog, for example, **AMI Creation with Aminator** (http://techblog.netflix.com/2013/03/ami-creation-with-aminator.html). They go really far with creating AMIs: there are multiple layers of them, each subsequent layer being baked from the AMI of the previous one. In the following diagram, taken from a Netflix blog, you can see what an application server AMI consists of, for example:

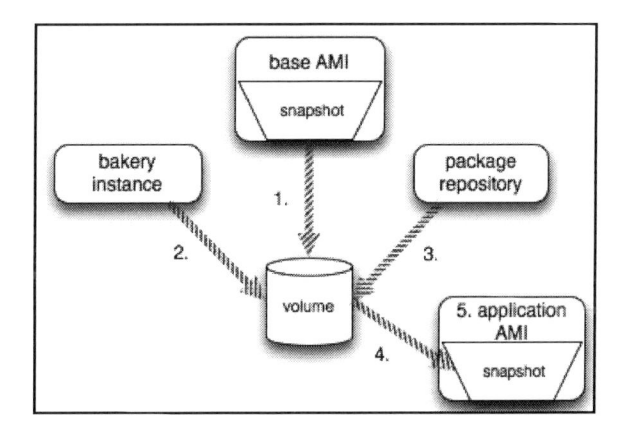

What becomes clear from reading the Netflix story, is that the transition to immutable infrastructure and baking a ton of images is not that straightforward. More than anything, immutable infrastructure requires a new set of tools and techniques to work well. Baking new images has to be fast, reliable, automated, and should be part of a continuous integration and continuous delivery pipeline. The process of rolling out new images is also different from the traditional configuration management approach. You just wait till chef-client or Puppet agent reruns in a few minutes to apply changes. In fact, an image becomes a new type of software package you develop, and it should be treated accordingly.

Another company that pushes the whole *throw away complete server and create a new one* approach hard is, don't be too surprised, HashiCorp. As already mentioned, Terraform works with replaceable servers in mind. The way it versions the `state` file works best with immutable servers. Just think about it for a moment: if we `taint` the provisioner as we did earlier, what kind of change will be recorded in a version control system? You might see the change to Puppet manifest, of course, but what if manifests and modules are coming from the different location, separate from the Terraform repository? Yes, you would see that `null_resource` was recreated, but that's about it. What was the reason behind the recreation? What's the new state of your infrastructure?

It's a whole different story if you replace the AMI ID. Now, you can clearly see that your machines were upgraded from AMI A to AMI B. You already know what changed between these two versions. You still have the full overview of the state and progress of your infrastructure. And look at the `aws_ami` data resource, built into Terraform - it is perhaps the most (if not only) robust and featureful data resource that Terraform has.

Of course, immutable infrastructure is just one way to look at infrastructure management. It's not the only way to do it, but it is certainly a viable alternative to the traditional approach. Lots of hugely successful technology companies are very happy without this approach. Just look at **Stack Overflow;** it has a handful of bare metal servers handling all the production traffic. No VMs, and no constant server replacement.

> Stack Overflow posts the full description of the state of their infrastructure every now and then. The latest state is documented in an article named *Stack Overflow: The Architecture - 2016 Edition.* Refer to `http://nickcraver.com/blog/2016/02/17/stack-overflow-the-architecture-2016-edition/`.

There are trade-offs to doing immutable infrastructure, such as added complexity to the whole toolset that you have for your operations team. It also can be much, much slower than just using configuration management. Baking an image is slow. Replacing it can also be slow. Certainly, it is really fast if you jump on the containers bandwagon, but this only means that you have to introduce another half a dozen new technologies to your organization.

None of this changes the fact that Terraform is a tool built with immutability in mind. And it's not the only tool: the HashiCorp stack has another utility that can be combined with Terraform in a powerful immutable infrastructure combo. This tool is named **Packer**, and you have to learn a bit of it if we want to master Terraform.

Baking images with Packer

Packer was released back in 2013 with the goal of simplifying, automating, and codifying the image creation process. It removes all the pain from baking images for different platforms by replacing many manual steps with a single JSON template fed to the CLI. It is written in the Go programming language, just like Terraform. Installing it is a piece of cake--just download the archive for your operating system from https://www.packer.io/downloads.html and extract the binary to a directory available in your $PATH environment variable. Then, verify your installation:

```
$> packer -v
0.12.0
```

You are all set up to bake images! To do so, just run `packer build my_template.json`. It won't work, of course, because we don't have a template yet. Create the `base.json` file and let's start filling it in. Our goal is to bake a CentOS 7 AMI with all packages updated and Puppet installed.

The only required section for the template is the **builders array definition**. Builders are configuration blocks of each provider that you want to bake an image for. Each provider is different, and each requires some kind of authorization to APIs, a few network details, and so on. Some example of builders are: AWS AMI, Google Compute Engine images, and VirtualBox. We will continue with using AWS. The `amazon-ebs` builder is what we are going to use. There are two other AWS builders in Packer that are more advanced and not required for our exercise.

Scaling and Updating Infrastructure

> Each Packer template can have multiple builders defined, which allows you to bake an image for multiple providers at once.

Configuration for the `amazon-ebs` builder looks as follows:

```
{
  "builders": [
    {
      "type": "amazon-ebs",
      "ami_name": "centos-7-base-puppet-{{timestamp}}",
      "region": "eu-central-1",
      "source_ami": "ami-9bf712f4",
      "instance_type": "t2.micro",
      "ssh_username": "centos",
      "ssh_pty": true
    }
  ]
}
```

If you don't have default VPC in your account, you will also need to specify the `vpc_id` and `subnet_id` keys. There is no need to configure a security group or a key pair if you don't want to: Packer will create them if they are not specified and destroy them after the build is done. Go ahead and start the build:

```
$> packer build base.json
amazon-ebs output will be in this color.
==> amazon-ebs: Prevalidating AMI Name...
    amazon-ebs: Found Image ID: ami-9bf712f4
==> amazon-ebs: Creating temporary keypair: packer_582c19ae-62d9-5ffd-06c3-ae22db9e7d3c
==> amazon-ebs: Creating temporary security group for this instance...
==> amazon-ebs: Authorizing access to port 22 the temporary security group...
==> amazon-ebs: Launching a source AWS instance...
    amazon-ebs: Instance ID: i-f00f954d
==> amazon-ebs: Waiting for instance (i-f00f954d) to become ready...
==> amazon-ebs: Waiting for SSH to become available...
==> amazon-ebs: Connected to SSH!
==> amazon-ebs: Stopping the source instance...
==> amazon-ebs: Waiting for the instance to stop...
==> amazon-ebs: Creating the AMI: centos-7-base-puppet-1479285166
    amazon-ebs: AMI: ami-a0d114cf
==> amazon-ebs: Waiting for AMI to become ready...
==> amazon-ebs: Terminating the source AWS instance...
==> amazon-ebs: Cleaning up any extra volumes...
```

```
==> amazon-ebs: Destroying volume (vol-52edcfd8)...
==> amazon-ebs: Deleting temporary security group...
==> amazon-ebs: Deleting temporary keypair...
Build 'amazon-ebs' finished.
==> Builds finished. The artifacts of successful builds are:
--> amazon-ebs: AMIs were created:
eu-central-1: ami-a0d114cf
```

If you read through this log, you will start appreciating the work Packer does. There are so many steps that would take tens of minutes to do by hand, only to create an AMI that is no different from the source image! With Packer, it's just 15 lines of JSON that you can put into source control, version it, and collaborate on it.

Note this part: `"ami_name": "centos-7-base-puppet-{{timestamp}}"`. Here, the internal Packer variable timestamp is used. It's very handy to name your AMIs. We could also define our own variables:

```
{
  "variables": {
    "environment": "production",
    "prefix": "{{ env `AMI_NAME_PREFIX` }}"
  },
  "builders": [
    {
      "ami_name": "{{ user `prefix` }}centos-7-base-puppet-{{ user `environment` }}-{{timestamp}}",
      "type": "amazon-ebs",
      ...
}
```

Just as with Terraform, there are many ways to supply these variables. You could do it inline:

```
$> packer build -var 'environment=development'
```

You could also store them in a file, as follows:

```
{
  "prefix": "packt"
}
```

Then, you could use it via a command-line argument:

```
$> packer build -var-file=variables.json
```

You could also send them via environment variables, if you configured the variable like the `"prefix"` variable shown earlier. To verify that the configuration was done correctly before running the build, you can use the `validate` command:

```
$> packer validate base.json
Template validated successfully.
```

Our template is pretty useless though: it just repackages the existing AMI! To do some real configuration of what goes into this AMI, we should use provisioners. Packer has been around for quite some time now, so it has much better support for the various provisioners than Terraform. It even has built-in Puppet provisioners (masterless and with Puppet server), two types of Ansible provisioners, Salt support, and many others. We will stick with the simple remote shell provisioner though. But I encourage you to try different ones out.

You can also configure multiple provisioners per each template. For example, you could upload configuration files with the file provisioner and then copy them to the necessary locations with a remote shell provisioner. It's not an uncommon use case: the file provisioner of Packer can't use `sudo` privileges, so if you need to upload a system service configuration, you need to do it in two steps. Add the following provisioner configuration right after builders:

```
...
],
  "provisioners": [
    {
      "type": "shell",
      "inline": [
        "sudo yum update -y",
        "sudo rpm -ivh http://yum.puppetlabs.com/puppetlabs-release-el-7.noarch.rpm",
        "sudo yum install puppet -y"
      ]
    }
  ]
```

Unfortunately, Packer doesn't have a substitute for the handy Terraform `plan` command. To test whether your template is working, you have to run the build. But, given that nonexisting AMI can't do much harm to the infrastructure, the only downside of it is cost--Packer creates EC2 instances in order to create the image, and these instances cost money.

Run `packer build base.json` again and get a cup of coffee--it takes a while for the build to finish. You probably won't want to do it manually in the future. Packer is perfect to be run inside a continuous integration server such as Jenkins or GitLab CI. Ideally, you should even try to architect the complete pipeline that builds the image, tests it, and rolls it out to production. But let's not overcomplicate things right now.

After a little while, Packer will report to you about the success of the build:

```
Build 'amazon-ebs' finished.
==> Builds finished. The artifacts of successful builds are:
--> amazon-ebs: AMIs were created:
eu-central-1: ami-12d3167d
```

With that, our Packer 101 is finished. Just like Terraform, the tools are focused on doing exactly one job, and it needs some tooling around it to make it productive. One option is to use HashiCorp Atlas--a paid service that wraps Packer and Terraform and provides hosting for your templates. Another option is, as usual, the DIY approach.

Again, you had to learn Packer a bit because that's the tool that works best when paired with Terraform. It's also the tool that makes immutable infrastructure efforts much more enjoyable. Without further ado, let's get back to Terraform and teach it how to update servers in an immutable fashion!

Rolling out AMI upgrades with Terraform

Remember that we used the data resource "aws_ami" to pull the latest AMI belonging to the AWS account configured in the template? At that time, we didn't put much effort into it, blindly pulling any existing AMI, as long as it was the latest updated one:

```
data "aws_ami" "app-ami" {
  most_recent = true
  owners = ["self"]
}
```

With Packer building our AMIs, we can put a bit more effort into this resource. We need to make sure that it pulls the image that is suitable for this application. First, simplify the Packer template: remove any variables and make sure that the "ami_name" key looks as simple as the following:

```
"ami_name": "centos-7-base-puppet-{{timestamp}}",
```

Scaling and Updating Infrastructure

Rebake the image and then modify the Terraform application module to use the following image:

```
data "aws_ami" "app-ami" {
  most_recent = true
  owners = ["self"]
  filter {
    name = "name"
    values = ["centos-7-base-puppet*"]
  }
}
```

From the `aws_instance` resource, we can now remove the provisioner: it was only installing Puppet on the machine, and we already have it installed inside the freshly baked AMI:

```
resource "aws_instance" "app-server" {
  ami = "${data.aws_ami.app-ami.id}"
  instance_type = "${lookup(var.instance_type, var.environment)}"
  subnet_id = "${element(var.subnets, count.index % 2)}"
  vpc_security_group_ids = ["${concat(var.extra_sgs,
  aws_security_group.allow_http.*.id)}"]
  user_data = "${data.template_file.user_data.rendered}"
  key_name = "${var.keypair}"
  tags {
    Name = "${var.name}"
  }
  count = "${var.instance_count}"
}
```

We are still keeping `user_data`, in case extra on-the-boot modifications to the server are required. Run the `terraform apply` command and make sure that you've destroyed all previously created resources by running the `terraform destroy` command. As a result, you will get two instances with an AMI created by Packer.

Now to the interesting part: what if we update the AMI? Rerun `packer build base.json`, give it a few minutes to run, and then execute the `terraform plan` command to see what Terraform is going to do now:

```
$> terraform plan
~ module.mighty_trousers.aws_elb.load-balancer
    instances.#: "" => "<computed>"
-/+ module.mighty_trousers.aws_instance.app-server.0
    ami:                           "ami-7f7fba10" => "ami-707cb91f"
(forces new resource)
    ....
-/+ module.mighty_trousers.aws_instance.app-server.1
```

```
      ami:                                    "ami-7f7fba10" => "ami-707cb91f"
 (forces new resource)
```

Apparently, our instances will be recreated because of the latest AMI change. Knowing the nature of Terraform, it will try to recreate them in parallel, leading to a possibly lengthy downtime. This is not what we consider a smooth update. So, how do we make it as painless as possible?

We talked about it in one of the initial chapters, but most likely you will have already forgotten about the life cycle block, specifically the `create_before_destroy` option. It will first create a new EC2 instance for us, and only then, it will remove the old one. Let's add it:

```
resource "aws_instance" "app-server" {
  ami = "${data.aws_ami.app-ami.id}"
  # ...
  count = "${var.instance_count}"
  lifecycle {
    create_before_destroy = true
  }
}
```

With this in place, the time required to switch AMIs will be much shorter. But it's still not perfect, because we could easily end up with two instances being unavailable simultaneously. It can be *okayish* for some applications, and it can be a complete disaster for others. What we should do is roll updates by replacing instances one by one. And that's where we are going to hit the limitations of Terraform pretty hard because it doesn't have an automated way to perform such upgrades.

Terraform allows you to apply only one resource using the `-target` argument. It is quite handy because it allows us to build a chain of commands, each of them changing only one instance, as follows:

```
$> terraform apply  -target "module.mighty_trousers.aws_instance.app-server[0]"
$> terraform apply  -target "module.mighty_trousers.aws_instance.app-server[1]"
```

It is handy, though, only if you have two, or maybe a dozen servers. More than 15 or 100? Good luck with doing this manually. We don't have to do it manually though. We can script it.

Scaling and Updating Infrastructure

As a most simplistic, dumb (and ugly) example, take a look at this tiny Ruby script:

```ruby
plan = 'terraform plan | grep "\\-/+ 
module.mighty_trousers.aws_instance.app-server"'

plan.split("\n").each do |line|
  line = line.gsub(/.+module/, "module")
  components = line.split(".")
  resource = "#{components[0..-2].join(".")}[#{components.last}]"
  puts terraform apply -target #{resource}'
end
```

This script will run the `Terraform plan` command and find all the instances that Terraform wants to replace and then loops through them, builds valid resource reference, and feeds it into the `terraform apply` command. As a result, instances will be replaced one by one, reducing the risk of downtime.

> This script leaves much to be desired, of course. It doesn't stream output from Terraform commands till execution is finished, as one example of its roughness.

After looking at this, even though it is smallest example script you might cry out in horror: *that's not the way I want to handle my infrastructure updates*. And you will be right screaming so. But as long as Terraform doesn't have handlers for update scenarios built in, you have to wrap it with extra tools and scripts, written in a scripting language you are most fond of.

Update scenarios are different depending on business, of course, so even if and when Terraform gets new features for updates, most likely, you will still have to come up with a tooling around it in order to make it fit your organization in the best way possible. It's a good idea to wrap common operations to your infrastructure operations in a **Makefile** inside your Terraform working directory.

There is another way to update your infrastructure: so-called blue-green deployments.

Performing blue-green deployments

The idea behind blue-green deployment is that, instead of updating existing instances of an application, you create a complete brand new production environment side by side with the existing one. Then, if it looks good, you switch the traffic to this new environment. If nothing breaks, you delete the old one. The new environment is called green, while the existing one is blue. As you might have guessed, the idea goes hand in hand with the immutable infrastructure concept and extends it beyond a single server to complete clusters of machines.

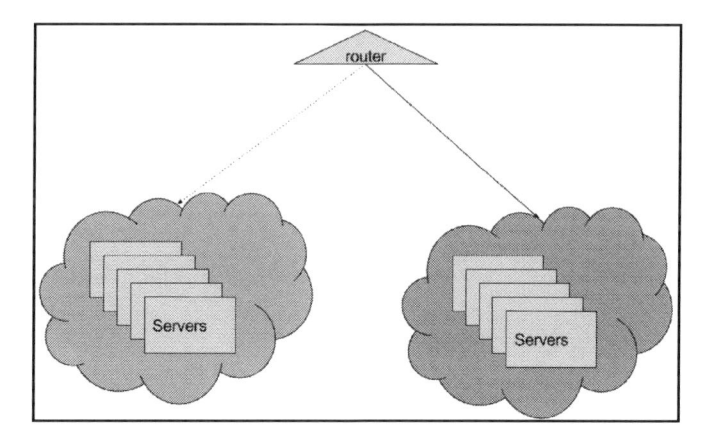

There are two ways to achieve this with Terraform:

- The manual approach
- The Auto Scaling groups approach

We will go with the first one. Doing things manually is not the best way to do things, but if you are in a non-AWS environment, you might not have a better choice. Elastic Load Balancer in our application module will play the role of the router in the preceding. We need to perform these steps:

1. Create a new group of instances
2. Switch traffic to the new group
3. Remove the old group

Start with copying over the configuration of `aws_instance.app-server`:

```
resource "aws_instance" "app-server-v2" {
  ami = "${data.aws_ami.app-ami.id}"
  # ...
}
```

Apply the template so Terraform creates this new group. After it has been created, you can verify that it works--run quick smoke tests, execute some Inspec tests, and so on. If it looks good, then it's time to switch traffic by modifying the ELB config:

```
resource "aws_elb" "load-balancer" {
  # ...
  instances = ["${aws_instance.app-server-v2.*.id}"]
  count = "${var.instance_count > 1 ? 1 : 0}"
}
```

Then, modify the provisioner:

```
resource "null_resource" "app_server_provisioner" {
  triggers {
    server_id = "${join(",", aws_instance.app-server-v2.*.id)}"
  }
  connection {
    user = "centos"
    host = "${element(aws_instance.app-server-v2.*.public_ip,
count.index)}"
  }
  # ...
}
```

It will take a few seconds to apply this change. Note that there is no interruption of the service: all traffic just started flowing to new instances of the `app-server-v2` group. It's time to destroy the old one by removing it from the module and applying the template again.

You could keep the name of the new instance group as `app-server-v2`, but it also could be rather confusing for people not aware of the update. We can easily rename it. First, do it inside the module template itself. Don't apply it just yet: it will destroy all instances because the `state` file is not aware of renaming. To rename it inside the `state` file, we can use the `terraform state mv` command:

```
$> terraform state mv module.mighty_trousers.aws_instance.app-server-v2
module.mighty_trousers.aws_instance.app-server
```

Scaling and Updating Infrastructure

Run the `terraform plan` command to verify that your instances are safe.

This approach works well if you don't use AWS or, for some reason, you avoid using Auto Scaling groups. There are a few manual steps, but as always, you can codify them relatively easily. If you do use AWS, and you don't mind learning yet another feature of it, then you might be much better off using Auto Scaling groups.

AWS **Auto Scaling groups** (**ASG**) allow you to adjust your infrastructure needs to the load. They can automatically increase in size as your usage grows and decrease back to a certain amount of machines when a traffic spike is gone. With ASG, you don't create instances by hand: you only need to specify launch configuration--consider it a template that an instance will be created from. In addition, ASG allows the configuring of scaling based on metrics from CloudWatch or **Simple Queue Service** (**SQS**). We won't use this feature though, as we are looking only for blue-green deployments implementation.

An Auto Scaling group can have ELB in front of it, so it balances all the traffic to instances in this group. If we want to implement blue-green deployment, we have to use it. This means that our previous attempt to save costs with automatic resolution of the need for ELB is going away:

```
resource "aws_elb" "load-balancer" {
  name = "application-load-balancer"
  subnets = ["${var.subnets}"]
  security_groups = ["${aws_security_group.allow_http.id}"]
  cross_zone_load_balancing = true
listener {
    instance_port = 80
    instance_protocol = "http"
    lb_port = 80
    lb_protocol = "http"
  }
  health_check {
    healthy_threshold = 2
    unhealthy_threshold = 2
    timeout = 3
    target = "TCP:80"
    interval = 30
  }
}
```

Remove the `aws_instance` configuration and replace it with launch configuration:

```
resource "aws_launch_configuration" "app-server" {
  image_id = "${data.aws_ami.app-ami.id}"
  instance_type = "${lookup(var.instance_type, var.environment)}"
```

```
    security_groups = ["${concat(var.extra_sgs,
aws_security_group.allow_http.*.id)}"]
    key_name = "${var.keypair}"

    user_data = "${data.template_file.user_data.rendered}"

    lifecycle {
      create_before_destroy = true
    }
}
```

Now we need to define Auto Scaling groups that use this launch configuration to figure out how to start instances:

```
resource "aws_autoscaling_group" "app-server" {
    vpc_zone_identifier = ["${var.subnets}"]
    name = "app-server-asg - ${aws_launch_configuration.app-server.name}"
    max_size = "${var.instance_count}"
    min_size = "${var.instance_count}"
    wait_for_elb_capacity = "${var.instance_count}"
    desired_capacity = "${var.instance_count}"
    health_check_grace_period = 300
    health_check_type = "ELB"
    launch_configuration = "${aws_launch_configuration.app-server.id}"
    load_balancers = ["${aws_elb.load-balancer.id}"]
    lifecycle {
      create_before_destroy = true
    }
}
```

Try to apply the template now, and you will note that Terraform waits for scaling group creation a bit too long. If you were to check the AWS Management Console, you would note that, although both instances and ASG are created, creation of ASG is not considered to be finished. This happens because instances fail health checks we defined for ELB. They fail because we removed the provisioner--we don't install Apache anymore, so there is no web server running on port 80!

Now, the real tricky part is that we cannot use Terraform provisioners if we use the ASG approach. Terraform can SSH only to machines it knows about, but it knows nothing about instances created through Auto Scaling groups. These instances are completely out of Terraform's control! It's even a bit sad, because that means a big part of our infrastructure is not managed as code: we only manage launch configuration and ASG with Terraform, but not actual servers.

Scaling and Updating Infrastructure

But it is also a good thing if we want to achieve immutable infrastructure: now we don't have any other choice except to replace complete machines. We could even remove a key pair attribute in order to launch configuration to ensure that instances are only replaced and not updated.

Eventually, Terraform will time out with the following error:

```
* aws_autoscaling_group.app-server: "app-server-asg -
terraform-20161121082119678053387ad": Waiting up to 10m0s: Need at least 2
healthy instances in ASG, have 1
```

We need to fix it, and there are multiple solutions to this problem:

- Edit user data to install Apache
- Recreate AMI with Packer, making Apache installation part of image baking
- Allow a configuration management tool to install it

Let's not bore ourselves with the second and third options and keep it simple. Make the `modules/application/user_data.sh.tpl` file look as follows:

```
#!/usr/bin/bash
yum install ${packages} -y
echo "${nameserver}" >> /etc/resolv.conf
cat << EOF > /tmp/setup.pp
package { 'httpd':
  ensure => installed
}
service { 'httpd':
  ensure  => running,
  require => [
    Package['httpd'],
  ],
}
EOF
puppet apply /tmp/setup.pp
```

We've embedded a complete Puppet manifest into our user data, so it will be run after the instance boot. If you run the `terraform plan` command, it will show you something like the following:

```
-/+ module.mighty_trousers.aws_autoscaling_group.app-server
      arn:                              "arn:aws:autoscaling:eu-
central-1:236110368157:autoScalingGroup:8da68b51-5793-453b-
a8fb-8b6cefc447b7:
autoScalingGroupName/app-server-asg - terraform-20161121082119678053387ad"
=>
```

[135]

```
        "<computed>"
            # ...
            name:                          "app-server-asg -
terraform-20161121082119678053387 2ad"
            => "<computed>" (forces new resource)
        -/+ module.mighty_trousers.aws_launch_configuration.app-server
            name:                          "terraform-20161121082119678053387 2ad"
            => "<computed>"
            # ...
            user_data:
"810cb11319ecdc0f8d9e8a373763ffbac105d184" =>
"e3aa616aef2387ebb482c6524aa996c436b74d5b" (forces new resource)
    Plan: 2 to add, 0 to change, 2 to destroy.
```

Changing user data forces launch configuration recreation. And changing the name of ASG forces recreation of ASG. It doesn't destroy ELB though, and now for the best part: remember we used `create_before_destroy` for Auto Scaling groups? Well, combined with `wait_for_elb_capacity`, we will get the following sequence from Terraform:

1. The new launch configuration is created
2. A new ASG is created
3. New ASG creates two new instances
4. The ASG is not considered created till both instances pass ELB health checks
5. Once they pass them, the old ASG is removed
6. Traffic flows to the new ASG!

See what's happening? Every time we change something to launch configuration, the change will roll out a form of completely new group of instances and traffic will be switched to those instances automatically once they pass health checks. It's exactly the same result we achieved with the manual approach earlier, but fully-automated and without any additional scripting from our side. That's how you do proper blue-green deployments on AWS with Terraform.

Of course, you have two downsides, already mentioned earlier:

- Your servers are not captured in code
- You cannot use Terraform provisioners any more

But if your use case benefits of blue-green deployment are greater than these two downsides, then Terraform will do the perfect job for you.

There is no way you can put ASG instances into your Terraform state. But what about other changes to your AWS infrastructure that are not managed by Terraform? There are two features of Terraform that can help here.

Refreshing infrastructure

It could be that someone updated the resource managed by Terraform manually, via AWS API or the AWS Management Console. If the changed attribute is specified inside the template, then you can fix it by running the `terraform apply` command--given that Terraform templates are the source of truth when it comes to the state of the infrastructure. But if this attribute is not managed by a Terraform template, then you might still want it to be reflected in your `state` file. That's when the `terraform refresh` command comes to the rescue.

Apply the template and then go to the AWS Console. Open the VPC section and find the VPC Terraform created. Right-click on this VPC and choose **Edit DNS Hostnames**. Then, change **DNS Hostnames** to **Yes**:

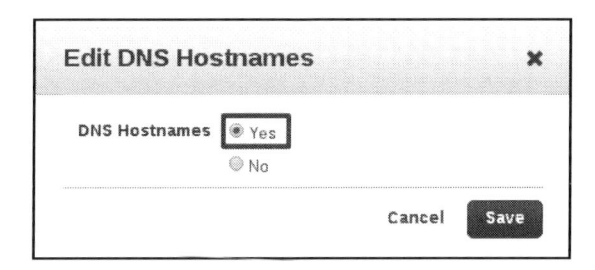

Now, head back to your console and execute the `terraform refresh` command. Open the `terraform.tfstate` file and verify that the change in the state file happened as expected:

```
"aws_vpc.my_vpc": {
    "type": "aws_vpc",
    "depends_on": [],
    "primary": {
        "id": "vpc-1d04fc75",
        "attributes": {
            ...
            "enable_dns_hostnames": "true",
```

Periodically running the `terraform refresh` command might be a good idea to ensure that the `state` file and actual infrastructure are in sync. But what if the resource was never part of the Terraform template?

Importing resources

Sometimes, resources are created manually. For example, you might have had an existing AWS infrastructure in place before you decided to introduce Terraform to your company. Now you need to move it somehow under Terraform's control. One option is, of course, to just recreate everything. Not all the resources are that easy to recreate though. That's where the `terraform import` command will help us.

If you destroyed it before, then rerun the template to create a new VPC. Then, create a new NAT gateway manually from the AWS Management Console:

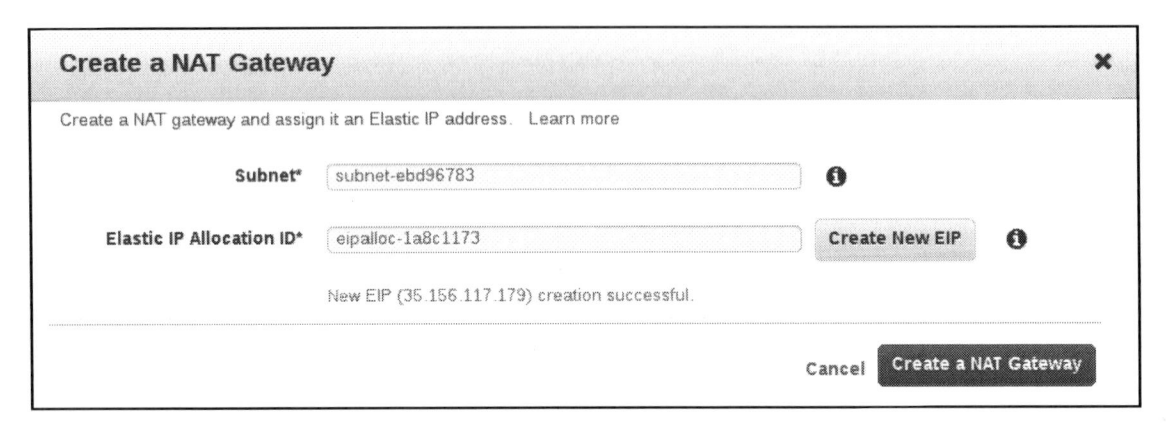

To import it, we need to know the ID of this gateway:

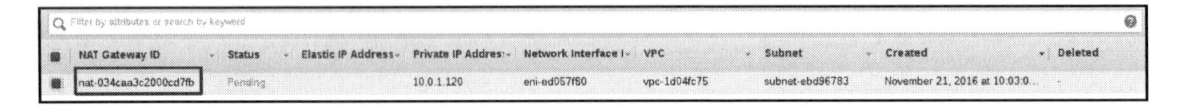

Copy it and go back to the console. To add this gateway to the `state` file, you need to execute the following command:

```
$> terraform import aws_nat_gateway.imported_gateway nat-034caa3c2000cd7fb
    provider.aws.region
    aws_nat_gateway.imported_gateway: Importing from ID "nat-034caa3c2000cd7fb"...
    aws_nat_gateway.imported_gateway: Import complete!
      Imported aws_nat_gateway (ID: nat-034caa3c2000cd7fb)
    aws_nat_gateway.imported_gateway: Refreshing state... (ID: nat-034caa3c2000cd7fb)
    Import success! The resources imported are shown above. These are
    now in your Terraform state. Import does not currently generate
```

Scaling and Updating Infrastructure

```
        configuration, so you must do this next. If you do not create
configuration
        for the above resources, then the next `terraform plan` will mark
        them for destruction.
```

Pay attention to what Terraform tells you at the end of the import procedure: import does NOT create configuration for this resource, it only adds it to the state file with the name you choose (imported_gateway in this case). If you don't add it to the template, then, during the next Terraform run, it will be destroyed. If you don't want it to be destroyed (and why would you), you have to add something similar to the following configuration to your template:

```
resource "aws_nat_gateway" "imported_gateway" {
  allocation_id = "eipalloc-1a8c1173"
  subnet_id = "${aws_subnet.private-1.id}"
  depends_on = ["aws_internet_gateway.gw"]
}
```

Importing like this can be useful if you have a really small amount of resources outside the Terraform template. If you have dozens of them, then this process might become a bit too repetitive and boring.

There is another solution: a Ruby gem named terraforming, which is capable of generating both state file and actual Terraform configurations. It is available on GitHub at https://github.com/dtan4/terraforming.

Installation is simple:

```
$> gem install terraforming
```

Now you can use the terraforming command to import various types of resources. Create VPC by hand and try it out:

```
$> terraforming vpc
resource "aws_vpc" "my-manual-vpc" {
    cidr_block           = "10.0.0.0/16"
    enable_dns_hostnames = false
    enable_dns_support   = true
    instance_tenancy     = "default"
    tags {
        "Name" = "my-manual-vpc"
    }
}
```

And to make terraforming return the possible `state` file for this `vpc`, run the following code:

```
terraforming vpc --tfstate
{
  "version": 1,
  "serial": 1,
  "modules": [
    {
      "path": [
        "root"
      ],
      "outputs": {
      },
      "resources": {
        "aws_vpc.my-manual-vpc ": {
```

Much more useful that built-in import command! It is capable of merging this `state` info into the existing `state` file as well:

```
$> terraforming vpc --state --merge=./terraform.tfstate
```

Note that `terraforming gem` works only with AWS resources. If you are using another provider, then the `terraform import` command is your last hope.

Summary

This was the longest and perhaps most important chapter so far! All these new infrastructure tools are useless if we don't know how to use them in production.

Now we know how to scale our Terraform resources with `count` and how to work around a lack of conditional statements in the HashiCorp Configuration Language with the help of the `count` property. You learned how to reference resources grouped with `count`, how to target them, and how to provision them properly. We also discovered a few more useful functions of Terraform.

Most importantly, you learned what immutable infrastructure is and what benefits it brings along to modern operations. With the theory in hand, we taught ourselves how to use yet another HashiCorp tool, Packer, and created a few AMIs with it. And, as we know that Terraform is perfect for immutable infrastructure, we took a deep look at multiple ways to do upgrades of complete instances. We did so manually, with self-written scripts, and we also used Auto Scaling groups of AWS. Finally, you also learned how to put existing infrastructure under Terraform's control with the `refresh` and `import` commands and an external `terraforming` utility.

It feels like we are all set up to rule the complete infrastructure with the help of Terraform, from development to production environments! There is one more thing though: it's a rare case that only one person works on everything in a company, thus, collaboration on infrastructure is also a very important topic that you should learn about. In the next chapter, we will figure out how to work with Terraform templates in a team, how to roll out updates without having conflicts with other people's work, and how to implement a complete continuous integration cycle for Terraform-managed infrastructure.

7
Collaborative Infrastructure

By this chapter, you've learned how to create and manage your infrastructure with Terraform. However, all the topics we have discussed apply only to a single-person operations department. If you are the only one using Terraform in your team, then you have all the knowledge already. Eventually, operations teams will reduce in size, and what required a dozen system admins in the past will require only a couple of them, the ones that are experienced in both operations and software development. Even then, it's not a single person, but at least a couple : having just one infrastructure engineer in a company is an example of a single point of failure.

And when you have multiple colleagues working on Terraform templates, you have a whole new package of problems to solve. How do you store your templates? How do you organize and split them? Where do you store them? And where do you store the `state` file? How do you roll out changes to production? And how do you test these changes?

That's what this chapter is going to be about. We will start from the basic setup. You will learn a bit of version control with Git, in case you are not familiar with it. We will proceed to different strategies for organizing templates. You will learn how to avoid conflicts when working with the `state` file and different approaches and tools in order to store it. We will also take a deep dive into Continuous Integration pipelines for templates, taking the whole *infrastructure as code* approach to its maximum. By the end of this chapter, you will be completely ready to introduce Terraform to your organization.

Version control with Git 101

> **TIP**: Feel free to skip this part if you are already familiar with version control and Git specifically.

Version Control System (**VCS**) simplifies work with constantly changing information, such as code. It allows us to store multiple versions of the same file, easily switch between them, and check who is responsible for which change. The most popular VCS today is Git, initially created to support Linux kernel development.

A VCS such as Git has many benefits:

- You have access to all versions of all files in the Git repository at any time; it's almost impossible to lose any part of a piece of code or a previous state of the code.
- Multiple developers can work on one project at the same time without interfering with each other's code and without fear of losing any changes made by colleagues. In Git, the possibilities of collaborative work are unlimited.

To create a repository, you've got to run `git init` in the `project` folder. To add files in it, first use `git add file_name` (or `git add .` to add all the files at once) and then `git commit -m 'description_of_changes_made'`. Any further changes in the files can also be done with `git add` and then you use `commit`. You can consider using `commit` to be the same thing as saving a version of the file.

Git has branches. You can work in a separate branch after creating it on the basis of the current one. By default, the main branch is the **master**. It is a best practice for big projects to develop a new feature in an individual branch, and when it's done, merge the changes into the main branch.

A `git` repository may have a remote copy. You can send commits there using `git push repository_name branch_name` and get them back with `git pull repository_name branch_name`.

This is how developers work on their computers and synchronize all the changes using a remote repository. In one picture, the simplified workflow looks as follows:

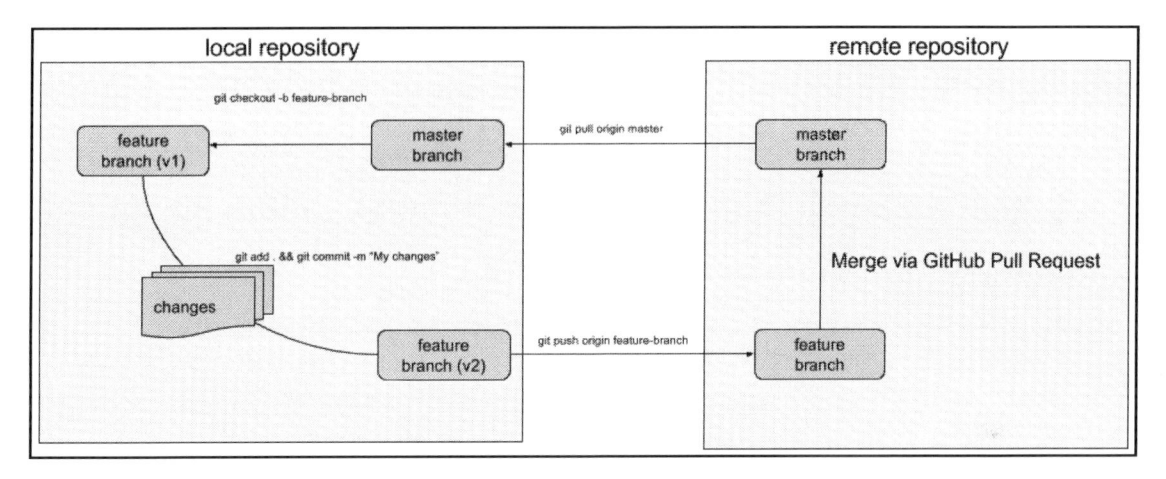

There are two repositories in sync in this image: the **local repository** and the **remote repository**. All work is done inside the **local repository**, as follows:

1. The developer creates a new branch from a master branch.
2. Commits changes to a new feature branch.
3. Pushes this branch to the remote repository.
4. After code review, this branch is merged into the master branch in the remote repository.
5. Finally, changes to the master branch are pulled to the local repository's master branch, and the cycle starts again.

There are multiple services, available in the form of *Software as a Service*, as well as enterprise-hosted software, that dramatically simplify all Git-related operations. Services like this provide remote hosting of Git repositories, mechanisms to collaborate on changes, and hundreds of integrations with other tools.

Undoubtedly, the most famous service like this is GitHub, where lots of open source projects are stored and maintained, including all HashiCorp products. GitHub revolutionized the way people work on open source, but it has a strong competition today in the form of **BitBucket** (widely used in enterprise environments) and **GitLab**.

Moving templates to Git

Traditionally, code in technical books uses GitHub for a good reason: everyone knows it, and it's free for open source (or just public) repositories. We are going to use GitLab though. First, it's free for both public and private projects. Second, it has some features that GitHub lacks, and we will need them for this chapter: more on this later.

> You could skip this section as well, but better if you don't. We will go through all the files that we have created in previous chapters and remove everything not needed.

This means that before proceeding further, you will need to get yourself an account at `https://about.gitlab.com/` (you can use your GitHub account to log in to GitLab with just few clicks).

> All code samples will still be available at `https://github.com/` as well.

We will start by doing a revision (see what I did there?) of all the files we have so far. All the code written previously in the book will be publicly available on GitLab.

Go to your directory and run `git init` to initialize a new Git repository. Let's check what Git wants us to add to the repository:

```
$> git status
On branch master
Initial commit
Untracked files:
  (use "git add <file>..." to include in what will be committed)
    .terraform/
    base.json
    development.tfvars
        custom_data_source.rb
    graph.png
    id_rsa.pub
    modules/
    playbook.yml
    rolling_update.rb
    specs/
    template.tf
    terraform.tfstate
    terraform.tfstate.backup
```

```
            variables.tf
    nothing added to commit but untracked files present (use "git add" to
track)
```

We decided to perform rolling updates with Auto Scaling groups, thus we don't need `rolling_update.rb` anymore. We've also switched to using only Puppet, which means `playbook.yml` needs to go too. Storing the graph image inside this repository is meaningless: throw it away as well. Also, remove the `specs/` folder: we will revise our approach to test servers later. We won't use an external data source, which means that `customer_data_source.rb` is obsolete.

As you might remember, Terraform *installs* local modules by making `symlink` to the `.terraform` directory. It should not be inside the Git repository. We can make it invisible for Git by creating the `.gitignore` file with the following content:

```
.terraform/
```

This is what the list of files for your first commit needs to look like:

- `.gitignore`
- `base.json`
- `development.tfvars`
- `id_rsa.pub`
- `modules/`
- `template.tf`
- `terraform.tfstate`
- `terraform.tfstate.backup`
- `variables.tf`

After this small cleanup, we can `commit` our command as follows:

```
$> git add .
$> git commit -m "Initial commit"
```

Now configure your `remote` repository and `push` it there:

```
$> git remote add origin git@gitlab.com:Fodoj/packt-terraform-book.git
$> git push origin master
```

You can get a link, such as `git@gitlab.com`, inside a GitLab web interface on the projects page. In the earlier example, `Fodoj` is the author's username and `packt-terraform-book` is the name of the repository.

Collaborative Infrastructure

Great! Now all the code we've written so far is version controlled! We can do changes to the template, run the `terraform apply` command, and `commit` it to the repository. Our colleagues can pull these changes and make their own changes as well. It's already so much better than what we had before.

Note that all the smaller steps will not be present in the `commit` history. You have to do them yourself if you really want to learn how to use Terraform.

> You can download it from the following repository if you were too lazy to write it yourself during the previous chapters: https://gitlab.com/Fodoj/packt-terraform-book/tree/master

Protecting secrets in a Git repository

Terraform doesn't provide any built-in way of securing your `state` file. Neither is there a way to secure only some part of it or even provide encrypted data inside your templates. And it's a shame because, sooner or later, you will have to use some kind of secrets with your templates: passwords, API keys, and others. If you plan to store your `state` file in the `git` repository, it's important to protect it. The easiest solution is to encrypt the whole `state` file, store the encrypted version in the repository, and distribute the key for decryption with your team members.

You could make this task easier with the help of a tool named `terrahelp`. Terrahelp is a small CLI written in Go that simplifies the encryption and decryption of your Terraform state files (and not only the `state` files). It has a nice integration with **Vault**, yet another HashiCorp tool, this time in order to manage secrets. Don't worry, we won't use Vault, it's rather a complex tool that deserves it's own book.

> Starting from version 0.8, Terraform has a built-in support for Vault as a source of data.

Download terrahelp binary from GitHub Releases at https://github.com/opencredo/terrahelp/releases, and make it available in your `$PATH`. Now you can use the `terrahelp encrypt` command to encrypt the complete `state` file like this:

```
$> terrahelp encrypt -file terraform.tfstate --simple-key AES256Key-32Characters0987654321
```

[148]

After you run it, your `terraform.tfstate` file will look similar to this:

```
@terrahelp-encrypted(90EYsi7dEgTqcwN63AePssKjIUF3nqJq4c9hFFnvNQ63eJwL0ZmMZL
8AUmUjsqCpho3af13DKjKTU3vQ8K8qMqgm70ToYBVYki6+8vq7nmPt5MGojhfPclAkrLmiestZ
SsTYVhmDbsykX/4zkCME29...many-more-symbols
```

The unencrypted version was put in a file named `terraform.tfstate.terrahelpbkp` for your convenience, in case you forget your encryption key. To avoid creating this file, add the `--nobackup` option:

```
$> terrahelp encrypt -file terraform.tfstate --simple-key
AES256Key-32Characters0987654321 --nobackup
```

The encrypted `state` file can be safely stored in a remote repository; only people who know the key (`AES256Key-32Characters0987654321`) will be able to decrypt it. The workflow for your Terraform procedure is the following:

1. Pull the latest changes from the `remote` repository.
2. Decrypt the `state` file.
3. Run the `terraform apply` command.
4. Encrypt the `state` file with the same key.

Many things can go wrong during this process. You could forget to encrypt the file and `push` the plain text to the repository. You could streamline this workflow by providing a good old `Makefile`, but it would not completely prevent bad things from happening. It would be much nicer to encrypt and decrypt `state` file automatically, without any additional actions from the developer who modifies the Terraform templates.

That's where a tool named `git-crypt` becomes very handy, as it implements exactly the mechanism just described. It's stored on GitHub at `https://github.com/AGWA/git-crypt` and written in C++. Sadly, there are not ready-to-use packages of `git-crypt`; we have to compile it ourselves.

> If you are a happy owner of Mac, then you can install `git-crypt` as `brew install git-crypt`.

Before installing, you should have a C++ compiler (for example, `gcc`), Make and OpenSSL development files (`libssl-dev` or `openssl-devel` package, depending on your Linux distribution) installed. You also need Git newer than 1.7.2. Installation is easy after all requirements are met:

```
$> git clone https://github.com/AGWA/git-crypt.git
$> cd git-crypt
$> make
$> sudo make install PREFIX=/usr/local
```

Verify successful installation with `git-crypt help` command.

> The version of `git-crypt` used for this chapter is `788a6a99f4289745e6bd12fae2ad8014af320a4f`. It's a `git commit` hash.

To configure `git-crypt` to manage the `state` file, we need to create a `.gitattributes` file in our repository with this content:

```
*.tfstate filter=git-crypt diff=git-crypt
*.tfstate.backup filter=git-crypt diff=git-crypt
```

Run `git-crypt init` at the root of Terraform repository. There are two ways you can use `git-crypt`: with a key shared among your colleagues or by encrypting data with the personal key of each colleague. You should use the second option, but for the purpose of this demonstration, we will stick with the first one. Somewhere, create a text file with a key in it (for example, generate it with the `ssh-keygen` command) and use this file to set up the encryption:

```
$> git-crypt export-key /path/to/secret/file
```

Because the `git commit` history already has the `state` file in it, you need to force encryption the first time you use `git-crypt`:

```
$> git-crypt status -f
```

Now add the changed `state` file and the backup of it to new `commit` and `push` them to your repository: you will note that it's impossible to see its contents on GitLab. If you clone the repository to your machine, the file will also be encrypted until you `unlock` it:

```
$> git-crypt unlock /path/to/secret/file
```

You need to do it just once. After the initial setup, your files will be automatically encrypted when you `commit` and `push` them and decrypted when you pull it from the `remote` repository. No chance of accidental plain text secret data commits! It's the same thing you would do with `terrahelp` and `Makefile`, but completely transparent.

Storing both the `templates` and `state` files in a `git` repository works well when you have just a few people working on them. You can always see who changed what in templates and the state of the infrastructure. Git is not the only state file storage supported by Terraform though. There are many other options for remote storage and other full APIs for working with them.

Storing state files remotely

As you know, by default, Terraform will store the `state` file on your local disk and you have to figure out yourself how to distribute it within your team. One option you learned is to store it in the `git` repository: you get the workflow, you get the versioning and you even get some level of security on top. But there is also a concept of **remote state** provided by Terraform.

The idea is that, before you start applying your templates, you configure a remote storage. After that, your `state` file will be pulled and pushed from a remote facility. There are 11 backends for your state provided by Terraform: Consul, S3, etcd, Atlas, and others. You will learn how to use **Simple Storage Service (S3)** for this purpose.

> Atlas is a commercial offering from HashiCorp. One part of it is named **Terraform Enterprise**: it combines secure remote state storage, versioning of state file changes, logs of Terraform runs, and some other features. It is well integrated with GitHub. You could use it as a ready-to-go solution, or you could keep reading this book to learn how to implement all these features yourself without spending any extra cash, and little to no time on implementation.

S3 is another AWS service. It's an object storage: you can throw into it as many files you like. Instagram uses it in order to store photographs, and many other companies use it for many other tasks. We will use it to store the Terraform `state` file. Why? Because it has many nice features, such as the following:

- Versioned buckets (more on this in a second)
- Flexible, powerful access controls

Collaborative Infrastructure

Storage on S3 is split into buckets: consider them as a separate disk (though it's not a completely correct analogy). Inside buckets, you can have folders (actually, there are no real folders on S3) and objects. Each object has a key: consider it as a filename. A bucket can be versioned; it means that all objects in this bucket will be stored as well and you can configure for how long they are stored and how many versions will remain.

Access to S3 is configured in the same way as any other AWS service: with **IAM** service. It allows you to set per-object permissions for a user in your AWS account, as well as a server role, and so on. Very powerful indeed.

Before using it with Terraform, we need to create a bucket, of course. You could create this bucket with Terraform itself, but that would become a bit of *a chicken and an egg problem*: if Terraform creates a bucket, then where is the state file for the template that creates this bucket stored? In another bucket? Oops, infinite loop.

Go to AWS console, choose S3 service, and create a bucket:

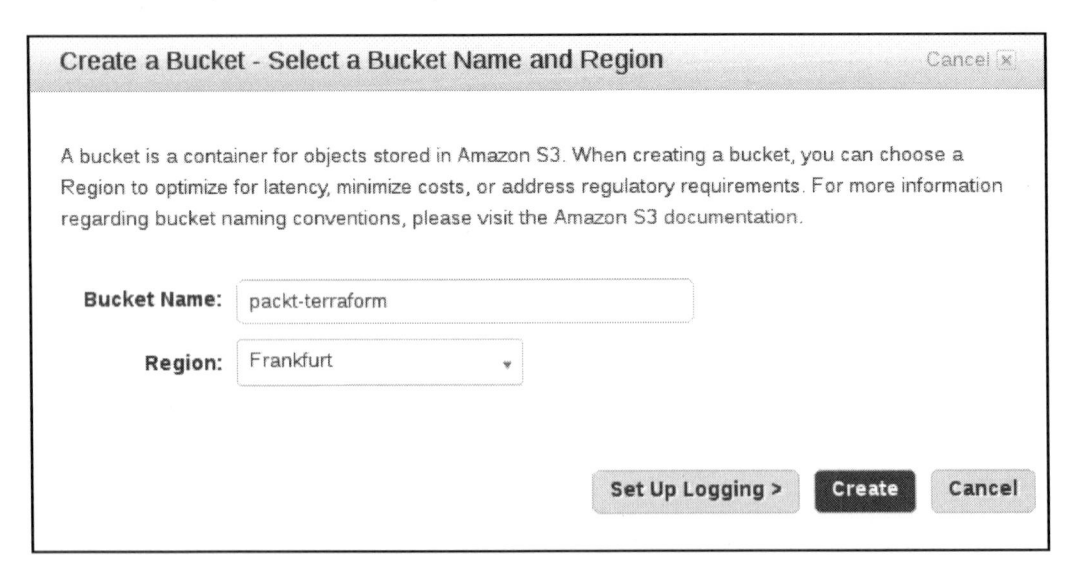

Don't click on **Create**! Instead, click on **Set up Logging** first: it will allow us to audit who accesses this bucket, performs which changes and when. You need a separate bucket for logs, so create it in advance in the same AWS region as the bucket. Note that bucket names are unique across AWS, so you won't be able to create a **packt-terraform** bucket.

Collaborative Infrastructure

Use a drop of imagination and pick the name yourself.

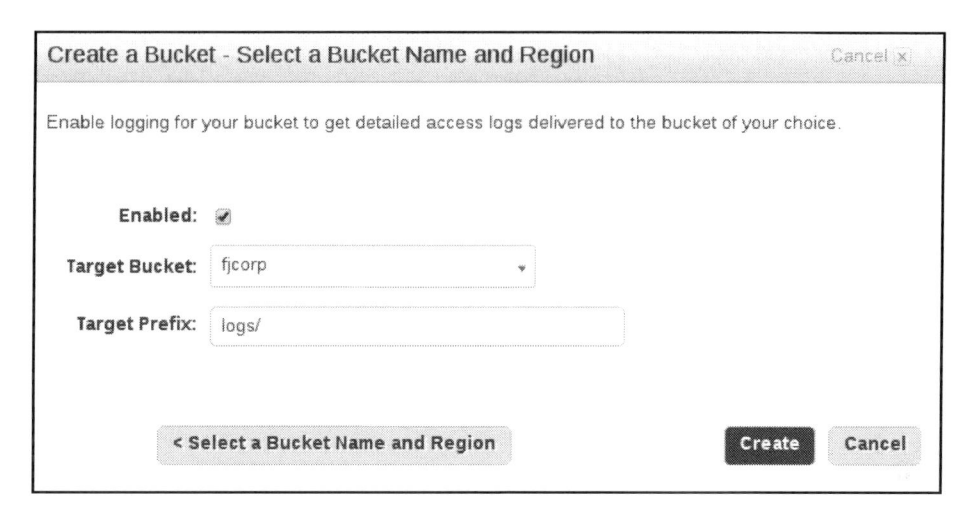

After the bucket is created, click on it in the bucket list and then click **Properties** at the top right. You need to select **Enable Versioning**:

Collaborative Infrastructure

After versioning is enabled, all versions of all objects in this bucket will be stored. It's a bit wasteful to store all the versions though. You probably don't care much about a `state` file version from half a year ago, and you don't want to pay to store it in S3. To solve this problem, create a new **Lifecycle Rules** for this bucket: the bucket is right under the **Versioning** tab in Properties. In the following screenshot, I chose to remove all versions older than one month:

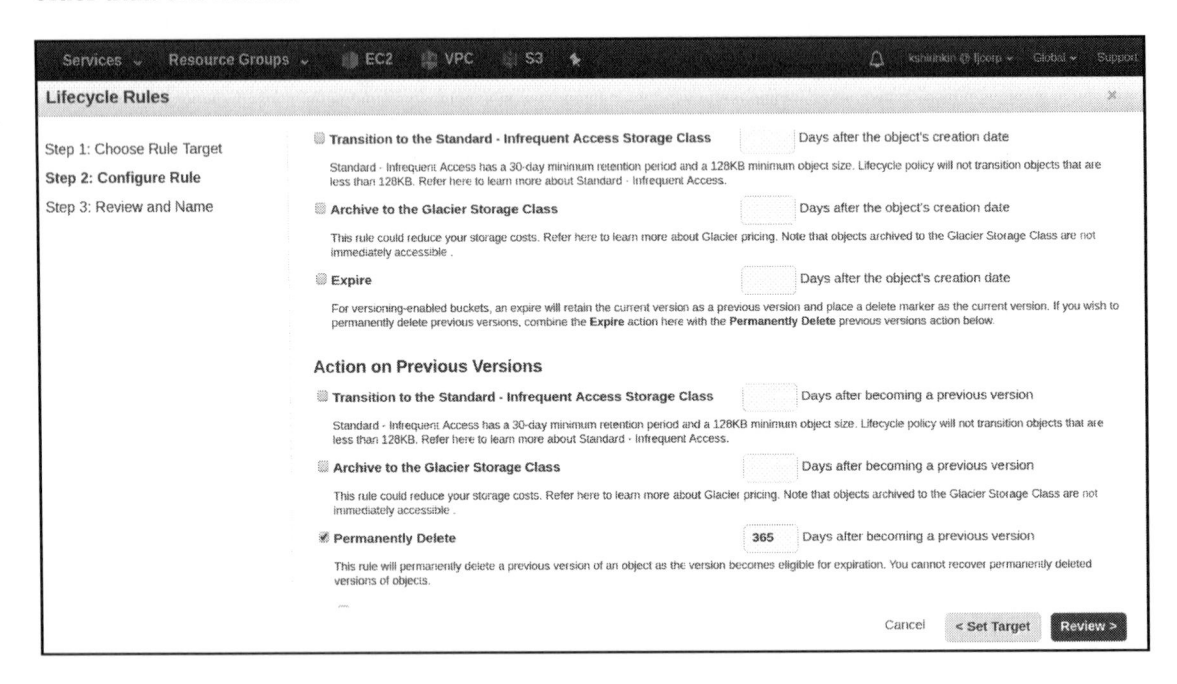

We are all set up to use this bucket as a remote state storage! Head back to your console, remove the existing `state` files, and run this command to enable the `remote` storage:

```
$> terraform remote config \
  -backend=s3 \
  -backend-config="bucket=packt-terraform" \
  -backend-config="key=mighty_trousers/
    terraform.tfstate" \
  -backend-config="region=eu-central-1"
Remote state management enabled
Remote state configured and pulled.
```

Note the `key` option: we can store multiple state files in the same bucket. Now go ahead and run the `terraform apply` command. After it is finished, your state file will be uploaded to S3 bucket. Run the `terraform destroy` command right after that just, so the new version is created on S3 and head to AWS console to verify that both versions are indeed stored (click on **Show** on the top to show the versions):

We have a remote versioned secure storage for state file decoupled from the `git` repository with actual Terraform templates!

> Even with `remote` storage, the `state` file is still cached locally on your machine inside the `.terraform` directory in your working directory.

Using S3 gives you a few extra benefits. For example, you could use events features that allow you to trigger some events on each change to a particular object or group of objects. Want to send notifications about the `state` file updates to the Slack channel? Easy.

S3 remote storage also gives you the benefit of an encrypted state file, which you can enable with the encrypt option. Try it out yourself as an exercise.

> I must admit that all of this is really easy to do with just GitLab/GitHub storage with Continuous Integration on top. But in the case of S3, you don't need to configure anything additional.

Connecting remote states together

Up until now, we naively stored all of our Terraform code in a single repository. We had a single template responsible for creating a network, routes, virtual machines, security groups, and everything else. It works pretty well, provided you have a single application with modest infrastructure around it. A single VPC, a few subnets, a small database, and a couple of instances: with this scale, there are few reasons to go beyond the single repository for all the infrastructure templates.

If you are part of a large organization, this approach can get you only so far. Companies that heavily rely on AWS tend to have dozens of use cases for many, various services. Only the IAM service has quite a few entities to manage: roles, policies, users, groups, and so on. Normally, there are many roles for different servers and even more policies for these roles. The network is also kind of complicated; at the very least, you would have one VPC per environment or even one per product per environment.

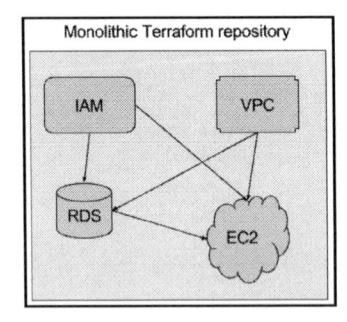

The problem becomes even more evident if there are multiple providers of infrastructure. While you might have your virtual machines on EC2, there could be other parts located elsewhere. For example, you could use a service different than the AWS Route53 DNS service, or some workloads could be located in a bare metal servers provider, such as Packet. All of this is hardly manageable via a single Terraform repository. There are two steps to make Terraform templates easy to maintain and reuse:

- Slice templates into different levels
- Build a collection of reusable modules

Once you note that your templates have grown fat and nasty, the first thing you should do is to slice them into different levels and then keep each level in a different repository and different `state` file. Configuration for services such as IAM is global for all AWS accounts, and it makes much more sense to manage it centrally, instead of spreading it over multiple repositories.

Collaborative Infrastructure

There is a special provider in Terraform named **Terraform Oops,** which has a data resource capable of fetching outputs from remote state files, and it works with all the remote storage backends that Terraform has. Let's learn how to use it by taking the IAM example described earlier. The IAM service is responsible for the fine-grained permissions setup for all AWS services for users, groups of users, and server roles. The last one is really important: on EC2, you should never use access keys to let servers talk to other AWS services. Instead, IAM roles must be used.

In addition, let's also refactor away the complete network setup. In the end, we will end up with something like this:

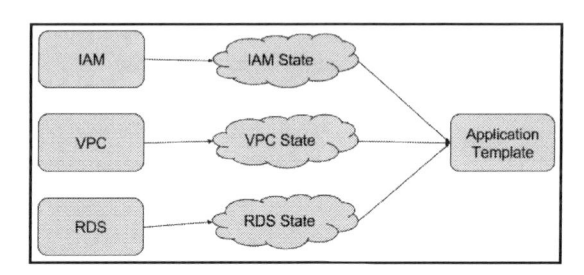

Note the **RDS (Relational Database Service)**. As an exercise, try to implement it yourself, after we are done with IAM and VPC.

Create another two folders on your machine: `packt-terraform-iam` and `packt-terraform-vpc`. Initialize a `git` repository in both of them. We will start with `packt-terraform-iam`. The final code will be available for download on GitLab at https://gitlab.com/Fodoj/packt-terraform-iam.

Create a folder named `policies`. That's where we are going to store all the JSON definitions of the various policies we have. Right inside, create a file named `cloudwatch=@put_metric.json` with the following content:

```
{
  "Version": "2012-10-17",
  "Statement": [
    {
      "Action": [
        "cloudwatch:PutMetric"
      ],
      "Effect": "Allow",
      "Resource": "*"
    }
  ]
}
```

Collaborative Infrastructure

This policy will allow us to put metrics to **CloudWatch**: monitoring and log service from AWS. If we want EC2 instance to use, we need to assign a role to it, and this role should have the policy mentioned earlier attached to it.

> Note the naming convention:
> `$serviceName=$resourveName@$actionName`. Thus makes it much easier to find out which policy does what just from the file name. This naming convention scales well for complex policies with dozens of lines of code.

In addition, we need a policy that allows the assumption of this role. Create another file `policies/sts=@assume_role.json`:

```
{
  "Version": "2012-10-17",
  "Statement": [
    {
      "Sid": "",
      "Effect": "Allow",
      "Principal": {
        "Service": "ec2.amazonaws.com"
      },
      "Action": "sts:AssumeRole"
    }
  ]
}
```

Now, let's write a template that creates a role, an instance profile, and `policy` for the role. It also returns the role name as an output; otherwise, we won't be able to retrieve it from the remote state:

```
resource "aws_iam_role" "base" {
  name = "base"
  assume_role_policy = "${file("./policies/sts=@assume_role.json")}"
}
resource "aws_iam_instance_profile" "base" {
  name = "base"
  roles = ["${aws_iam_role.base.name}"]
}
resource "aws_iam_policy" "cloudwatch-put-metric" {
  name = "cloudwatch=@put_metric"
  policy = "${file("./policies/cloudwatch=@put_metric.json")}"
}
resource "aws_iam_policy_attachment" "cloudwatch-put-metric-attachment" {
  name = "cloudwatch=@put_metric attachment"
  roles = [ "${aws_iam_role.base.name}" ]
  policy_arn = "${aws_iam_policy.cloudwatch-put-metric.arn}"
```

[158]

```
}
output "base-role-name" {
  value = "${aws_iam_role.base.name}"
}
```

Do *NOT* apply this template yet. We need the state to be stored remotely, so first of all configure the remote storage using the same S3 bucket:

```
terraform remote config \
    -backend=s3 \
    -backend-config="bucket=packt-terraform" \
    -backend-config="key=iam/terraform.tfstate" \
    -backend-config="region=eu-central-1"
```

Now you can apply the template. Note that even though IAM is a global service, Terraform will still ask you for the AWS region.

We have a remote state that can be used inside the *MightyTrousers* application! Add a new variable to the application module, name it `iam_role`, and use inside the launch configuration. Then, inside `template.tf`, just before invoking the module, add this configuration:

```
data "terraform_remote_state" "iam" {
    backend = "s3"
    config {
        bucket = "packt-terraform"
        key = iam/terraform.tfstate
        region = eu-central-1
    }
}
```

Then pass it to the module:

```
module "mighty_trousers" {
  source = "./modules/application"
  # ...
  iam_role = "${data.terraform_remote_state.iam.base-role-name}"
}
```

It's done! You can verify that the role name is pulled from the remote state by running the `terraform plan` command. Now it's time to move the network away as well. The final code is on GitLab at `https://gitlab.com/Fodoj/packt-terraform-vpc`.

Collaborative Infrastructure

Move the `vpc_cidr` and `subnet_cidr` variables from `variables.tf` to a new repository `packt-terraform-vpc` in the new `variables.tf` file. Then, simply move all VPC configuration: VPC, subnets, route table, and Internet gateway to the `packt-terraform-vpc/template.tf` file. Finally, add a few outputs for this template:

```
output "public-subnet-1-id" {
  value = "${aws_subnet.public-1.id}"
}
output "public-subnet-2-id" {
  value = "${aws_subnet.public-2.id}"
}
output "vpc_id" {
  value = "${aws_vpc.my-vpc.id}"
}
```

Don't forget to configure the `remote` destination:

```
terraform remote config \
    -backend=s3 \
    -backend-config="bucket=packt-terraform" \
    -backend-config="key=vpc/terraform.tfstate" \
    -backend-config="region=eu-central-1"
```

Once again, apply the template and head back to *MightyTrousers*. Add another data source:

```
data "terraform_remote_state" "vpc" {
  backend = "s3"
  config {
    bucket = "packt-terraform"
    key = "vpc/terraform.tfstate"
    region = "eu-central-1"
  }
}
```

Use this data source inside the module:

```
module "mighty_trousers" {
  source = "./modules/application"
  vpc_id = "${data.terraform_remote_state.vpc.vpc_id}"
  subnets = [            "${data.terraform_remote_state.vpc.public-subnet-1-id}",            "${data.terraform_remote_state.vpc.public-subnet-2-id}"  ]    # ..
}
```

Don't forget to update the default security group to use remote `vpc_id` as well.

We've decoupled IAM and VPC management from the application template completely. Developers can focus on the template for the software they write and AWS administrators can design and update network and permissions in parallel.

Developers are not exposed to this level of configuration if administrators don't want them to be. In the background, the IAM and VPC repositories can grow a lot by adding more and more policies, roles, users, and networks. All these changes will be invisible to the authors of the application template, as long as remote states of the IAM and VPC repositories still return outputs it expects.

We've slimmed down an application template a lot, but there is still a big piece of code that doesn't really belong to the application template repository: the application module itself.

Storing modules remotely

We've stored the application module in the very same directory where our main Terraform template resides. It makes it impossible to reuse: if there is a new application in the company that requires the same infrastructure (meaning the same module), then we cannot easily use it.

Remember the source attribute of the module?

```
module "mighty_trousers" {
  source = "./modules/application"
```

Well, it turns out that it doesn't have to be a path to a local directory. In fact, there are multiple supported sources for modules:

- GitHub
- BitBucket
- Generic Git and Mercurial repositories
- HTTP URLs
- S3 buckets

Storing modules in one of these destinations allows us to have a collection of reusable components. We can even version our modules, just like system packages or programming language libraries.

As we are deep into GitLab already, let's create yet another repository and call it packt-terraform-app-module. As always, all the code written in this chapter is available on GitLab at https://gitlab.com/Fodoj/packt-terraform-app-module.

Collaborative Infrastructure

Move everything inside the `./modules/application/` folder to `packt-terraform-app-module` and `commit` it. Then, remove the modules directory from the *MightyTrousers* project completely and specify the path to the remote `module` as follows:

```
module "mighty_trousers" {
    source = "git::https://gitlab.com/Fodoj/packt-terraform-app-module.git"
    vpc_id = "${data.terraform_remote_state.vpc.vpc_id}"
      # ...
}
```

Replace the URL with your `git` repository (or just use the one previously specified, if you were too lazy to complete the exercise). Finally, run the `terraform get` command to pull the module. It will be stored inside the `.terraform/` directory: now it makes more sense than `symlink` to a local directory.

It's a bad idea to reference master branch of a remote module because it can change at any moment. Let's tag the module with version 0.1 and reference it inside `template.tf`:

```
# from packt-terraform-app-module
$> git tag v0.1
$> git push origin master :tags
```

Reference the earlier module in `template.tf`:

```
module "mighty_trousers" {
    source =
"git::https://gitlab.com/Fodoj/packt-terraform-app-module.git?ref=v0.1"
    vpc_id = "${data.terraform_remote_state.vpc.vpc_id}"
      # ...
}
```

Our `packt-terraform` repository, dedicated to the *MightyTrousers* application, is so tiny now. The main template is just 60 lines long, and it simply pulls some data from remote state files and configures a module, also stored remotely. If we want to add a new application, we can create a similar repository without almost any effort. Developers can work with application repository. Owners of modules collection can focus on their modules repositories. Administrators are free to change the global VPC and IAM configuration. This is an infrastructure collaboration dream come true.

Yet we still have one problem left to solve: locking of `state` file.

Locking state files with Terragrunt

Let's say you have your application template and a team of five people working on it. One Monday morning you decide to change a minor thing, such as the security group, and at the same time your colleague, sitting in a room next to you, decides to change a disk size for instances. Being confident that you are the only ones running the `terraform apply` command at this moment, you both do `terraform apply`, `push` changed `state` file to the `git` repository (or to remote storage like S3), and end up in a total disaster.

If your `state` file is stored in `git`, then you will meet the `merge` conflict: not too bad, you can try to resolve it by hand, and you will still be able to see who changed what. If you use a remote backend for the `state` file, then things are going south. Which `state` file is now inside the remote storage? And where do the changes of another Terraform run go?

It is dangerous to work on the same state file in a team, because there is no locking out of the box. You could pay for Atlas, which gives you this feature, but what if you don't want to pay for Atlas, for many obvious reasons? Well, there are a few (if not many) solutions to this problem.

The first one that we will take a look at is **Terragrunt**. Terragrunt is a thin wrapper for Terraform that supports locking of the Terraform state and enforces best practices. The GitHub page of this is yet another open source CLI wrapper for Terraform. It solves two problems, outlined as the following:

- Provides a locking mechanism
- Forces you to use remote state, always

Locking in Terragrunt is provided via DynamoDB: a NoSQL database service from AWS. Let's go ahead and install it.

> Grab the latest version from GitHub Releases at `https://github.com/gruntwork-io/terragrunt/releases`. Make it available in your `$PATH`. On Mac, you can install Terragrunt by running `brew install terragrunt`

Collaborative Infrastructure

To start using it, create a `.terragrunt` file in the `packt-terraform` repository. This file uses the already familiar HCL language (the same language Terraform templates are written in). It is needed to configure remote storage for your state file and locking. As we already have remote storage configured, carefully use the existing configuration inside this new file:

```
lock = {
  backend = "dynamodb"
  config {
    state_file_id = "mighty_trousers"
  }
}
remote_state = {
  backend = "s3"
  config {
    bucket = "packt-terraform"
    key = "mighty_trousers/terraform.tfstate"
    region = "eu-central-1"
  }
}
```

Instead of using the `terraform` commands, you should use `terragrunt` now: `terragrunt get/plan/apply/destroy/output`. You will note this fact when you run apply for the first time:

```
[terragrunt] 2016/12/01 09:52:58 Reading Terragrunt config file at .terragrunt
[terragrunt] 2016/12/01 09:52:58 Remote state is already configured for backend s3
[terragrunt] 2016/12/01 09:52:58 Attempting to acquire lock for state file mighty_trousers in DynamoDB
[terragrunt] 2016/12/01 09:52:58 Lock table terragrunt_locks does not exist in DynamoDB.
Will need to create it just this first time.
[terragrunt] 2016/12/01 09:52:58 Creating table terragrunt_locks in DynamoDB
[terragrunt] 2016/12/01 09:52:59 Table terragrunt_locks is not yet in active state.
Will check again after 10s.
[terragrunt] 2016/12/01 09:53:09 Success! Table terragrunt_locks is now in active state.
[terragrunt] 2016/12/01 09:53:09 Attempting to create lock item for state file mighty_trousers
in DynamoDB table terragrunt_locks
[terragrunt] 2016/12/01 09:53:10 Lock acquired!
```

Let's make an experiment and run the `terragrunt apply` command twice. Open a new tab in your terminal, start the `terragrunt run` command in the first one, then switch to the second one, and start it again. You won't be able to proceed because the first tab already acquired a lock for the `state` file:

```
[terragrunt] 2016/12/01 09:54:37 Reading Terragrunt config file at
.terragrunt
[terragrunt] 2016/12/01 09:54:37 Remote state is already configured for
backend s3
[terragrunt] 2016/12/01 09:54:37 Attempting to acquire lock for state file
mighty_trousers in DynamoDB
[terragrunt] 2016/12/01 09:54:38 Attempting to create lock item for state
file
mighty_trousers in DynamoDB table terragrunt_locks
[terragrunt] 2016/12/01 09:54:39 Someone already has a lock on state file
mighty_trousers! AIDAJP2R36AIB5ZY25DEQ@192.168.178.21 acquired the lock on
2016-12-01 08:53:10.237944107 +0000 UTC.
[terragrunt] 2016/12/01 09:54:39 Will try to acquire lock again in 10s.
```

This is a real game-changer for your Terraform operations: no more conflicts much more predictability! The locking in Terragrunt works by creating (if one does not exist) a new table in DynamoDB, as well as a new item in this table with the name of the `state_file_id` option value. This item will contain useful metadata about the lock, such as who created it and when. After the Terraform run is finished, the item is removed from the table, making a `state` file available for modifications again.

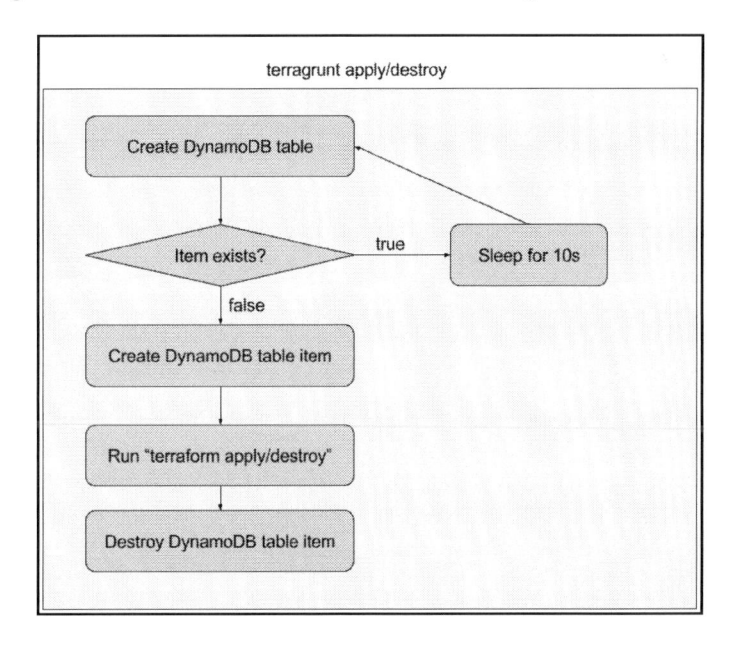

[165]

Collaborative Infrastructure

The process of locking is not really complicated. Terragrunt supports DynamoDB as a backend, but you could implement a similar solution yourself. For example, you could create a `Makefile` that wraps around Terraform the same way Terragrunt does and implement locking with a simple file on S3 or in some other way, as per convenience for your organization name. You will actually need to do it if you do not rely on AWS as your infrastructure provider.

With Terragrunt, you can also acquire the lock manually, for a longer period of time:

```
$> terragrunt acquire-lock
[terragrunt] 2016/12/01 11:16:46 Reading Terragrunt config file at
.terragrunt
Are you sure you want to acquire a long-term lock? (y/n) y
[terragrunt] 2016/12/01 11:16:49 Acquiring long-term lock. To release the
lock,
use the release-lock command.
[terragrunt] 2016/12/01 11:16:49 Attempting to acquire lock for state file
mighty_trousers in DynamoDB
[terragrunt] 2016/12/01 11:16:50 Attempting to create lock item for state
file
mighty_trousers in DynamoDB table terragrunt_locks
[terragrunt] 2016/12/01 11:16:51 Lock acquired!
```

After you are done Terraforming, just run `terragrunt release-lock`.

Terragrunt is a lifesaver for any Terraform user; with a few simple features, it makes collaboration on Terraform-related work much more robust, predictable and production-ready. The company behind Terragrunt heavily relies on Terraform for its operations, so one can expect this tool to be further supported and improved with new features.

As mentioned though, the locking features of Terragrunt work only if you are ready to use AWS DynamoDB, which might not always be the case. You could implement locking yourself and hope that it works well, and your team members might follow all procedures as expected. But there is still the possibility of a human mistake. We can keep it at a minimum by completely removing the right to run `terraform apply` command from the operators' and developers' machines. How would it run, then? CI, of course.

Moving infrastructure updates to the CI pipeline

Remember how we started this book with a discussion of *infrastructure as code* concepts? Well, if we want to go further treating infrastructure as a real code, then we could (and even should) apply all the same best practices currently existing in software development, and Continuous Integration is a big part of it. The idea behind CI (in case you missed all the buzz about it a few years ago) is to be able to test, build, and deploy your code regularly and automatically. The way it works is by using special software that takes care of all the tasks of making your software ready for production. You only need to define which tasks exactly are part of your CI and how to execute them.

Do you remember that we chose GitLab over GitHub due to some features that GitHub lacks? The most important feature that GitLab has completely integrated into all development workflows and that GitHub doesn't have at all, is GitLab CI. Yes, you can use Travis CI or Jenkins or anything else with GitHub, but that will mean that you need to support an extra tool. With GitLab, you have CI in place from day one, ready to be used for any of your repositories, and for free. GitLab CI has fewer features than, let's say, Jenkins, and as of now it can be tricky to implement complex pipelines with it, but for simpler use cases, especially where there are few dependencies between different components, it's perfect.

CI builds in GitLab run inside GitLab Runners: these are any machines that you've configured to be able to run builds. GitLab (`https://about.gitlab.com/`), a free hosted version of GitLab, provides these runners for free (via a partnership with DigitalOcean, a VPS hosting company) and we are going to use them. Let's take a look at this picture:

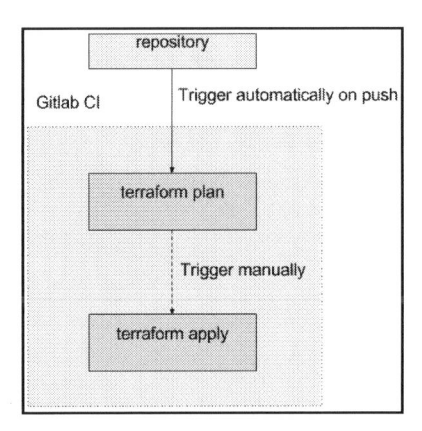

Collaborative Infrastructure

Our goal for now is to only run the `terraform plan` command in CI on every change and makes the `apply` step manual. If we were to run `apply` automatically as well--for example, on each merge to the master branch--then we would also achieve the continuous delivery setup. Being able to do it for infrastructure depends a lot on what kind of updates you perform and how much you trust the tool to do it. What if five uull requests (or merge requests) merged and applied one after another. Would this completely break your whole AWS setup? Production deployments of changes to Terraform templates are better being performed manually, but nothing stops you from doing it automatically for staging environments.

Let's get back to the `packt-terraform-book` repository, because that's the one that actually has the deployed code in it. In order to enable GitLab CI, we simply need to add the `.gitlab-ci.yml` file to the repository. This file will specify all the builds stages and steps that we need to take. Create this file with the following content:

```
image: alpine:latest
test:
  script:
    - echo "Terraform!"
```

Then `push` it to GitLab. If you open the GitLab web interface and click on the **Pipelines** tab, you will notice that there is one pipeline running with one stage test in it. This step doesn't do anything useful just yet, but we have our CI up and running just by adding a single file!

Pay attention to the first line that specifies the image key: by default, GitLab runs all the builds inside Docker containers, and in this case, we told it to run the Alpine Linux container. Alpine is a very lightweight Linux distribution with zero overhead. It's very fast to start and use, but it also requires you to preinstall more tools by yourself.

Luckily, the tools we are going to use are written in Go, which means that they are normally distributed as precompiled binaries. Still, to download and unpack these tools, we need at least `curl` and `unzip` programs. And to download the remote modules, we need Git and SSH. Let's install these tools and then install Terraform and Terragrunt:

```
before_script:
  - apk add --update curl unzip git openssh
  - curl -O https://releases.hashicorp.com/terraform/0.7.13/terraform_0.7.13_linux_amd64.zip
  - unzip terraform_0.7.13_linux_amd64.zip
  - curl -LO https://github.com/gruntwork-io/terragrunt/releases/download/v0.6.2/terragrunt_linux_386
  - mv terragrunt_linux_386 terragrunt
  - chmod +x terragrunt
```

```
test:
  script:
    - ./terraform -v
    - ./terragrunt -v
```

It takes roughly 50 seconds each time we run a build just to download and install the required packages. Any CI tool allows us to use some kind of cache for these operations. GitLab CI is not an exception here, and you can play around with its cache features as an exercise. For this example, though, we will leave it as it is and proceed to actually using our template.

Make sure that the `.terragrunt` file looks like this (except for the S3 bucket name; this is going to be different if you run it yourself):

```
lock = {
  backend = "dynamodb"
  config {
    state_file_id = "mighty_trousers"
  }
}
remote_state = {
  backend = "s3"
  config {
    bucket = "packt-terraform"
    key = "mighty_trousers/terraform.tfstate"
    region = "eu-central-1"
  }
}
```

If we try to run the `terragrunt plan` command in GitLab CI, it won't work. That's because we did not configure the GitLab CI to be able to talk to AWS APIs. If we were running our own GitLab CI Runners on top of EC2, then we would use IAM roles to provide access to these APIs. But as we are using free runners on top of the Digital Ocean, we have to provide access keys. We should not use our personal keys: let's create a separate service user in AWS IAM and generate keys for it.

Collaborative Infrastructure

Open the users tab in the IAM interface and click on **Add another user**. Then, fill in the name of the user and make sure that you tick the **Programmatic access** checkbox:

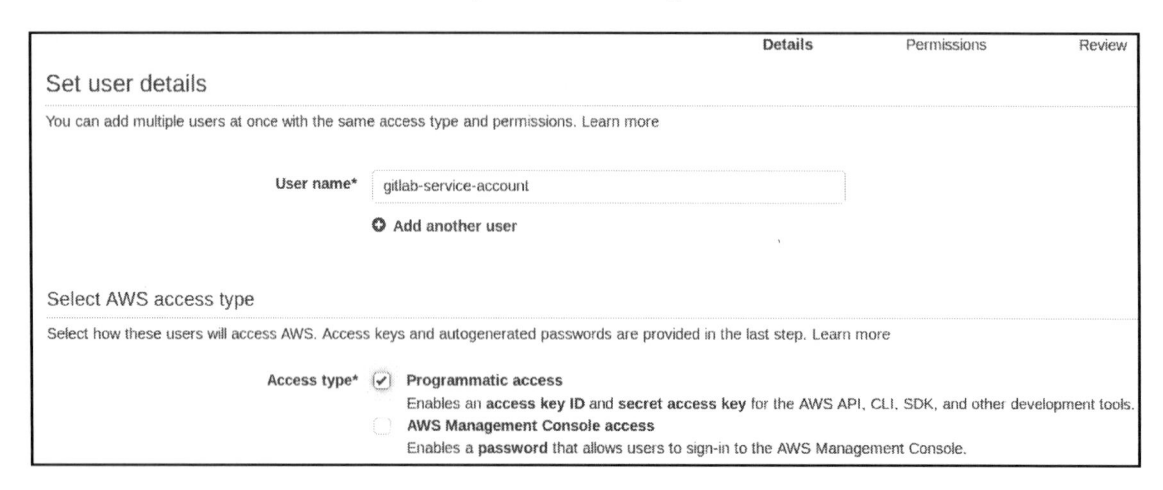

	Details	Permissions	Review

Set user details

You can add multiple users at once with the same access type and permissions. Learn more

User name*: gitlab-service-account

⊕ Add another user

Select AWS access type

Select how these users will access AWS. Access keys and autogenerated passwords are provided in the last step. Learn more

Access type*:
- ✓ **Programmatic access**
  Enables an **access key ID** and **secret access key** for the AWS API, CLI, SDK, and other development tools.
- ☐ **AWS Management Console access**
  Enables a **password** that allows users to sign-in to the AWS Management Console.

Give this user full permission to EC2, VPC, DynamoDB (for Terragrunt lock), S3 (for remote storage access), and IAM. You will be right if you say that these are too broad a set of permissions. In the real world, you should narrow them down to only a small set of essential policies.

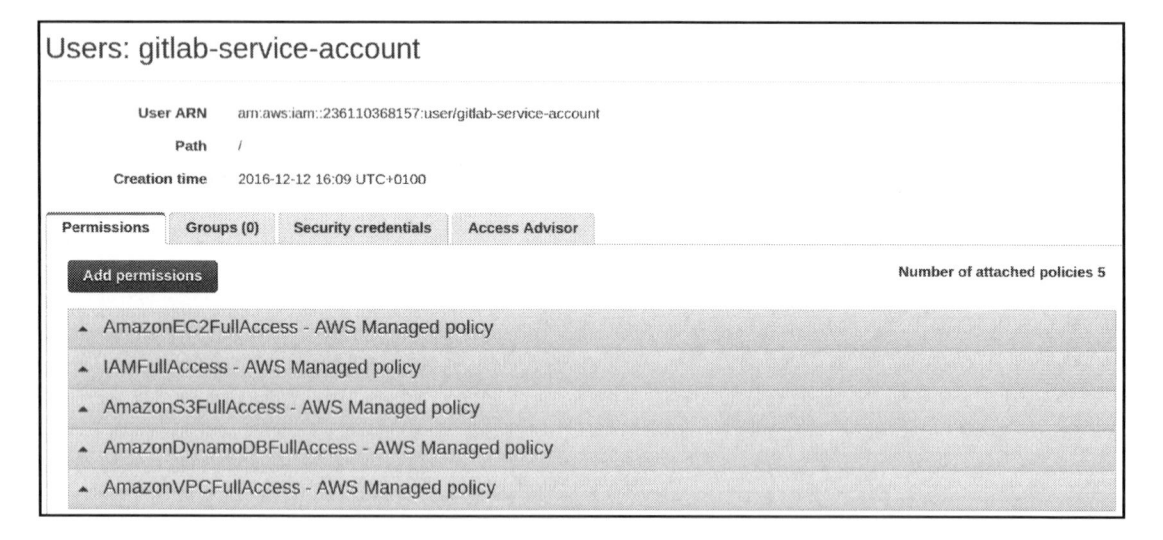

Users: gitlab-service-account

User ARN: arn:aws:iam::236110368157:user/gitlab-service-account
Path: /
Creation time: 2016-12-12 16:09 UTC+0100

| Permissions | Groups (0) | Security credentials | Access Advisor |

Add permissions   Number of attached policies 5

- AmazonEC2FullAccess - AWS Managed policy
- IAMFullAccess - AWS Managed policy
- AmazonS3FullAccess - AWS Managed policy
- AmazonDynamoDBFullAccess - AWS Managed policy
- AmazonVPCFullAccess - AWS Managed policy

After creating a user, AWS will show you secret and access keys for it. We need to use them inside GitLab. Go to the **Variables** section of settings page and define two new variables, **AWS_ACCESS_KEY_ID** and **AWS_SECRET_ACCESS_KEY**, with the values that AWS just gave to you:

These variables will be available as environment variables inside GitLab CI builds. As Terraform picks AWS variables for access and secret keys automatically, we can hope that GitLab CI is now ready to execute Terraform runs. Modify the `test` stage steps in `.gitlab-ci.yml` to look like this:

```
test:
  script:
    - export PATH=$PATH:$(pwd)
    - ./terragrunt plan
```

Push this change to GitLab, head to the GitLab **Pipelines** view and observe what happens next.

Collaborative Infrastructure

> If you have issues with access to AWS, make sure that variables on GitLab do not have any empty spaces before or after their values. GitLab doesn't strip them for you.

If everything has been set up correctly, then you will get a plan of what Terraform would do:

This is pretty awesome, if you think about it for a moment. All of your infrastructure code is stored and versioned securely in the `git` repository. All your changes are planned and presented in a nice UI, right inside the same tool you use for code storage. What is missing is an **Apply** state. Let's add it to `.gitlab-ci.yml` and mark it as manual. We should refactor this file a bit as well:

```
plan:
  stage: "test"
  script:
    - export PATH=$PATH:$(pwd)
    - ./terragrunt plan

apply:
  stage: "deploy"
  when: "manual"
  only: ["master"]
  script:
    - export PATH=$PATH:$(pwd)
    - ./terragrunt apply
```

After you `push` it, GitLab will start the pipeline, and it will also present each stage in a nice graph:

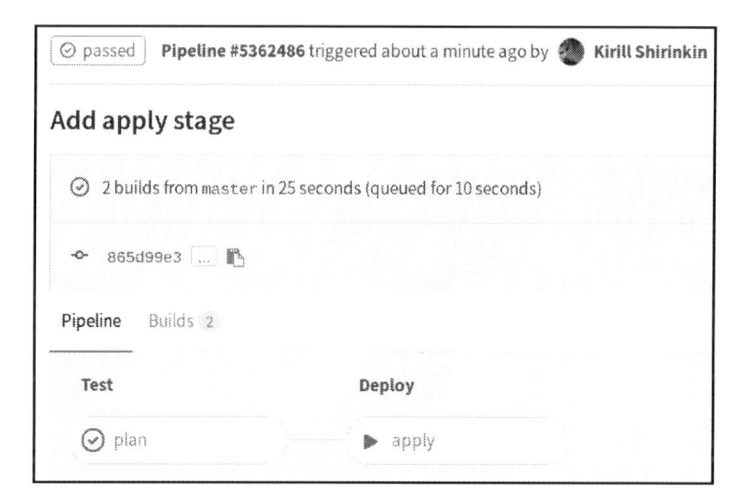

After carefully examining the **plan** (or test) stage, you can trigger the **apply** manually and watch GitLab CI doing it. The `state` file will be stored in S3, still available to you if you have to do Terraform tasks locally. By using Terragrunt, you ensure that no one else is running the `terraform apply` command at this moment; the state is locked via Terragrunt and DynamoDB. We also marked the **apply** stage to be available only on the **master** branch, so it's impossible to trigger it for a pull request.

As a result, once a colleague of yours makes a new pull request, the **plan** stage will be executed. A person with the privilege to merge this pull request can review both changes to the template and the result of the **plan** stage, and if everything looks fine, merge it with master, watch the **plan** stage again, and then manually trigger **apply**. It's a Continuous Integration, only for your infrastructure.

Collaborative Infrastructure

Trigger the **apply** stage, wait for it to complete, and then trigger the whole pipeline manually from the GitLab interface:

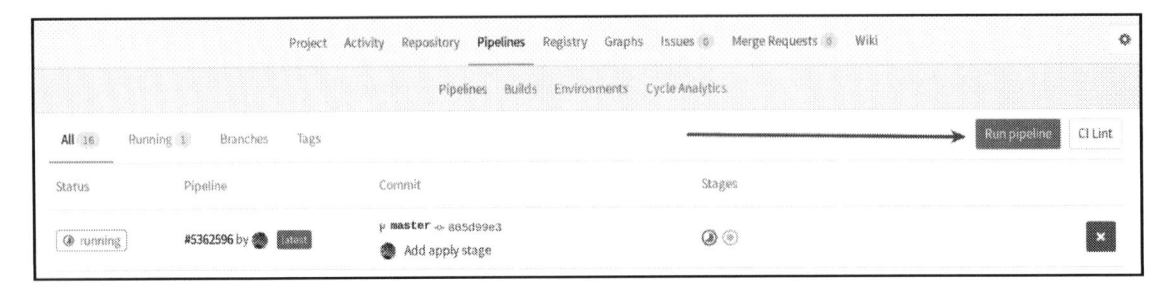

![GitLab pipelines interface showing a running pipeline #5362596 on master branch with Add apply stage commit, and a Run pipeline button highlighted]

The **plan** stage should report that there is nothing to change now. Destroy it from your local machine with the `terragrunt destroy` command to avoid losing money on the stack just created.

The GitLab CI and Terraform combination is just one of many possible ones, depending on your choice of source code control and CI/CD tool. You can achieve the same with many other tools, and you will get the same, pretty nice result: an ability to treat your infrastructure as a complete deliverable software component, versioned with SCM and built and deployed with CI. Managing production infrastructure this way is only one (though already highly beneficial) application of this workflow. We could come up with many other ones.

For example, we could create review apps with Terraform. Review apps are something you create for each pull request to be able to do QA on every feature: sometimes expensive, but always nice thing to have. Terraform could take care of creating complete production-like infrastructure for every review application, and then another pipeline step could deploy the actual code to this infrastructure, and then sending a notification to the QA team to verify that the feature was implemented as expected. And after the review is done? Use the `terraform destroy` command to destroy it!

> Initially, review apps were promoted by Heroku, but the whole idea is so nice that it doesn't have to depend on Heroku. Tools such as Terraform make it trivial to implement it yourself in a few short steps.

You could also build a complete self-service tool for your organization that allows anyone to create complete environments with a few clicks, removes all the struggle of managing state file, thinks about Terraform templates, and so on. During the creation of a tool like this at one client of this book author, the final service was proudly named **TerrorFarm**, as a combination of *farm of servers and terraform*, of course (and a bit of a terror, due to unpredictable nature of some Terraform applications).

Integration testing of Terraform modules

In one of the previous chapters on making various tools play well with Terraform, we already took a quick look at running infrastructure tests. Back then we used Inspec to run a test against the single EC2 instance. A few chapters forward, and now we have much more complex Terraform setup on our hands; one that is split across four repositories.

If we were to consider ourselves old-fashioned traditional system administrators, we would be quite happy with what we have achieved by now. But a good software developer (and if we are doing infrastructure as code, then we are already software developers, regardless of our previous experience) would never leave any code without proper tests. And what we wrote in the past is nothing like a proper test.

But what should we test? We must not run tests against the production environment (the one we just configured GitLab CI for), and it is meaningless to test VPC and IAM repositories in isolation. So the only good (really good) candidate for integration tests is the application module we wrote earlier. How about we create an integration test, located in the application module repository, that would spin up an instance of this module, connect it to existing VPC and IAM configuration, and verify that it really does start a web application (the base Apache web server, in this case)?

Perhaps the most popular tool to run infrastructure tests these days is **TestKitchen**. The idea behind TestKitchen is to make running these kind of tests very simple: you only need to write a single `YAML` configuration file that defines how to create machines (using `driver`) and how to test them (using `verifier`). After configuring, you can create, test, and destroy servers with a single `kitchen test` command. Initially, it was built to work with Chef, but now it has many instance of `driver` and `verifier`, distributed as Ruby gems. And you guessed right; there is a `kitchen-terraform` plugin. Let's learn how to use it.

Collaborative Infrastructure

Navigate to the `packt-terraform-app-module` repository and create `Gemfile` over there with these contents:

```
source 'https://rubygems.org/'
ruby '2.3.1'
gem 'test-kitchen'
gem 'kitchen-terraform'
```

You need Ruby, `rubygems` and `bundler gem` installed before you proceed. Once you have them, simply run the `bundle install` command to install `test-kitchen` and its Terraform plugin. `kitchen-terraform` handles all the `terraform get`, `terraform apply`, and `terraform destroy` for us; we only need to create a template that it will handle. Create a `test` directory inside a module repository and add `.kitchen.yml` inside it. Be careful: it's important not to add it to the `root` folder of the module because, in that case, TestKitchen will try to apply the module template itself, and not a template that uses module inside it.

First of all, we need to define a driver inside this file:

```
---
driver:
  name: terraform
```

It's Terraform. This means that `kitchen-terraform` will be used. Next goes the `provisioner`. Normally, `driver` is responsible for creating machines (Docker, EC2, and others) and the `provisioner` for how to provision them (Chef, Puppet, and Ansible). In case of Terraform, we are interested only in creating, and provisioning is configured somewhere inside the Terraform templates. Because of this, the only provisioner we configure is Terraform itself:

```
provisioner:
  name: terraform
```

Normally, if you test a server configuration, you would want to test it for multiple platforms, such as Red Hat Linux, Debian, and so on. Again, it makes little sense in the context of Terraform. Still, TestKitchen requires us to define a platform, so let's make it happy:

```
platforms:
  - name: centos
```

The `transport` section is responsible for connecting to the machines created by TestKitchen. Generate a dummy key-pair inside the `test` folder and configure `transport` as follows:

```
transport:
  name: ssh
  ssh_key: ./test/id_rsa
```

`suites` is a set of tests to run. We will define just one:

```
suites:
  - name: default
```

Finally, `verifier` is what TestKitchen will run to make sure that the server (or infrastructure, in our case) was created and configured correctly:

```
verifier:
  name: shell
  command: ./test.sh
  sleep: 180
```

There are multiple verifiers available, including one already familiar to us, Inspec. Lots of them are focused on testing one particular server. But when we talk about the whole infrastructure, we can't test just one server: we need to somehow verify all of it. It is especially true for our application module because it doesn't create the server directly: instead it creates an Auto-scaling groups and exposes only an endpoint that all the servers hide behind. That's why we are using `shell verifier` which invokes a script on the machine you run tests from: inside this script, we have full flexibility of what to test. If the script returns 1, the test has failed; if 0, it succeeded. In the case of an application module that only creates a bunch of statelesss web servers running Apache in default configuration, the whole test can consist of a check to see whether the ELB endpoint returns a standard Apache page or not:

```bash
#!/bin/bash
cd .kitchen/kitchen-terraform/$KITCHEN_SUITE-$KITCHEN_PLATFORM
hostname=$(terraform output app_endpoint)
res=$(curl $hostname | grep "Testing 123" | wc -c)
if [[ $res = "0" ]]
then
  exit 1
else
  exit 0
fi
```

This example is kept intentionally simple, of course. It's up to you how complex you make this test. It can even, for example, run the complete Selenium-based set of tests for a complex web application. It all depends on what exactly Terraform creates. Note this weird line:

```
cd .kitchen/kitchen-terraform/$KITCHEN_SUITE-$KITCHEN_PLATFORM
```

When you run TestKitchen, it stores the Terraform `state` file in a local `.kitchen/kitchen-terraform` directory, divided by `suites` and `platforms`. The name of the suite and a platform is available via the environment variable in any script configured for `shell verifier`.

The only thing missing now is an actual test Terraform template. It's not much different from what we used in a `production` repository earlier, except that behind the curtains some of the variables were removed. As an exercise, modify the module itself to fit the following template:

```
# ...
module "test_app" {
   source = "../"
   vpc_id = "${data.terraform_remote_state.vpc.vpc_id}"
   subnets = [
              "${data.terraform_remote_state.vpc.public-subnet-1-id}",
              "${data.terraform_remote_state.vpc.public-subnet-2-id}"
             ]
   name = "TestApp"
   keypair = "${aws_key_pair.terraform.key_name}"
   environment = "${var.environment}"
   extra_sgs = ["${aws_security_group.default.id}"]
   instance_count = 1
   iam_role = "${data.terraform_remote_state.iam.base-role-name}"
}
output "app_endpoint" {
   value = "${module.test_app.app_address}"
}
```

It still uses the same remote state files for IAM and VPC configuration; no need to change anything there. `instance_count` was changed to just 1 : we don't want our tests to be too expensive. To run these tests, we only need to run the `bundle exec kitchen test` command. This command will do this:

1. Apply the Terraform template and put the `state` file to `.kitchen`.
2. Execute the `test.sh` script.
3. Destroy the Terraform environments.

For a small template that we have will take roughly three minutes to create all of the infrastructure and then another few minutes for Puppet to do its job: hence `sleep: 180` option for `verifier`. Clearly you want to run these tests inside a Continuous Integration server instead of doing it manually.

We looked at `shell verifier`, but `kitchen-terraform` has an extra `verifier` built-in. This `verifier` is nothing but a wrapper around Inspec, and it expects you to provide a set of IP addresses or DNS names to SSH to. For `shell verifier`, we wrote that we don't really need transport section, but it was left in intentionally as the first step for you to try `terraform verifier` out.

As a final, more difficult exercise for you to verify what you've learned about Terraform and all its related tools, do the following:

1. Create a new Terraform module that creates two servers: App server and DB server.
2. Write an integration test with `kitchen-terraform` that tests both of these servers.
3. Set up a CI pipeline to run this test (pick the CI tool you like most).
4. Add an extra stage to this pipeline to deploy a production environment with Terragrunt and S3 remote storage.

If you can do this, then you've mastered Terraform and infrastructure as code.

Summary

It's been another long chapter to digest and there has been a ton of new things to learn and try. You started by learning Git and how to organize work though Git branches, remote repositories, and code review. You learned how to easily store secrets in a setup like this with `git-crypt`. After this, we took a look at the remote storage of state files for Terraform, and at various methods to split the Terraform code inside the organization.

As part of this, we wrote our first completely remote Terraform module, refactored the whole IAM and VPC management away from the main repository, and connected it all nicely in a small, and clean template. To avoid conflicts and to better structure the infrastructure work, we set up the Terragrunt utility and learned how to use it too.

We took the whole infrastructure as code idea to the extreme by introducing a complete Continuous Integration pipeline for the infrastructure (and learned a bit of GitLab CI). As a final battle, we even created a real integration test suite for the Terraform code.

There is not much else to learn about the use of Terraform at this point. In the next chapter, we will summarize all you have learned about Terraform in this book and reflect a bit on the future of this tool.

8
Future of Terraform

You've learned Terraform! No, seriously, you have. You might (we hope) still be busy doing the final big exercise from the end of the previous chapter. That's alright -- it's not a simple one and it takes time.

We have finished covering everything that is there to learn about this fancy new (relatively new) HashiCorp tool. In this chapter, you won't see many code samples, diagrams, or logs. Instead, we are going to recap what you've learned, talk about some pros and cons of introducing Terraform to your organization, and speculate about the future of this utility. Don't skip this chapter, especially the recap sections! It will have a lot of useful tips, as well as references to books and articles that will help you to dive deeper into each particular topic related to Terraform usage. These were not included in the chapters themselves in order to focus on learning Terraform and not to spread attention between dozens of things.

Infrastructure as code and Terraform replacements

We just went through six chapters of intense coding. It is easy to forget what it was all about a hundred pages ago, so let's quickly summarize the journey we are almost through with.

Chapter 1, *Infrastructure Automation*, was not entirely about Terraform -- you learned a few general principles of modern infrastructure automation and, more importantly, you got to learn what **Infrastructure as Code (IaC)** is. If you want to be successful in doing modern operations, understanding IaC in depth is a must. This book only covers one particular tool, so you need to do some extra reading to really master the ideas behind IaC. Perhaps the most comprehensive work on this topic is a book titled *Infrastructure as Code: Managing Servers in The Cloud* by Kief Morris.

In addition, check out *Infrastructure as Code (IAC) Cookbook* by Stephane Jourdan and Pierre Pomes, which has many practical examples of different IaC tools, including Terraform.

That very first chapter also listed some requirements to a tool such as Terraform. Terraform is not the only tool of this kind though. It is important to know alternatives and to consider each of them for your particular use case. Here is a list of the most important technologies in this area; investigate each of them at least a bit:

- CloudFormation, for AWS environments
- Heat, for OpenStack environments
- Chef provisioning, for Chef-heavy environments
- Various Puppet modules, if you rely on Puppet a lot (look for the `puppetlabs-aws` module as a starting point)
- `SparkleFormation`, the new tool that covers all major cloud providers and builds on top of native cloud templating services such as `CloudFormation`

Learning AWS and compiling Terraform

`Chapter 2`, *Deploying First Server*, was not only about installing Terraform, but it also taught a bit about AWS basics. If you want to use Terraform with AWS only, then you first need to know AWS, of course. AWS has very detailed documentation and a lot of examples in it -- it's the best place to start learning it. There are also probably hundreds of books about it. For a beginner, something like *Learning AWS* by Aurobindo Sarkar and Amit Shah will fit best.

It's easy to install the official version of Terraform. Sometimes, though, you will want to use the edge version, not yet released. The Terraform README has a good explanation of how to compile it: https://github.com/hashicorp/terraform#developing-terraform. What is important to know is that it is totally fine to use the edge version of Terraform. Trust me, many big organizations do it, simply because they need some new features already now, and they can't wait an extra couple of months till the official release. Compile the binary, upload it to an internal artifact repository (could be just an S3 bucket) and use your own. Just try not to get stuck with a self-compiled version for too long.

Learning Consul

In `Chapter 4`, *Storing and Supplying Configuration,* we took a brief look at Consul, a service discovery tool from HashiCorp. We did not use it much because it deserves its own book itself. Nevertheless, Consul still should be seriously considered for configuration data storage for Terraform. There are many examples already out there on the Internet telling how Consul works in production environments. As usual, start with the official documentation, then explore whether Consul Template can improve your configuration management efforts and, finally, Google some blog posts about it, such as the excellent coverage from Data Dog: *Consul at DataDog* (`https://engineering.datadoghq.com/consul-at-datadog/`).

Provisioning and configuration management

In `Chapter 5`, *Connecting with Other Tools,* you learned how to connect Terraform with various existing infrastructure tools. We've spent a lot of time on configuration management systems in particular. It is a popular thing to say these days that configuration management tools are not required any longer and immutable infrastructure, containers, or whatever is the best and only practice. Some people on the Internet even argue that you can replace Chef and Puppet only with Terraform. Certainly, that's not the case. Even though you could indeed replace Terraform with Chef or Puppet.

Terraform covers only one level of infrastructure (as discussed in `Chapter 1`, *Infrastructure Automation*), and it does it reasonably well. For everything that goes inside a particular piece of hardware (or virtual hardware), you need a proper configuration management tool, regardless of whether you need to configure an EC2 instance, a big bare metal server, or networking hardware. If you have thousands of machines, the benefits of Chef or Puppet become even more clear. So, do yourself a favor and learn at least one of them, then combine it with Terraform to achieve infrastructure excellence at every layer of your environments.

Immutable infrastructure

Terraform works best if you adapt Immutable Infrastructure principles. It can also work pretty well if you use containers. Read *Rebuilding our* infrastructure (`https://segment.com/blog/rebuilding-our-infrastructure/`) from Segment about how they used Terraform with AWS Elastic Container Service and Docker for the new version of their infrastructure. It has good examples in the Continuous Integration part as well.

Future of Terraform

The ECS plus Terraform approach seems to gain higher adoption in general; for example, check out a presentation about more or less the same idea by Yevgeniy Brikman, named *Infrastructure as Code: Running microservices on AWS with Docker, Terraform, and ECS* (`http://www.ybrikman.com/writing/2016/03/31/infrastructure-as-code-microservices-aws-docker-terraform-ecs/`).

Finally, there is a really good blog post by Simone Gotti about rolling upgrades with Terraform. Simone also published all the code to perform such upgrades, so you can easily use it. He published on Immutable Infrastructure with Terraform and rolling upgrades of stateful services on the following links:

- `https://sgotti.me/post/terraform-immutable-infrastructure-stateful-rolling-upgrades/`
- `https://github.com/sorintlab/terraform-immutable-upgrades`

Be careful with this approach though -- all the containers, stories are still pretty fresh and have some not-yet-solved problems, especially in the operations area. Experiment wisely.

Collaboration and CI/CD

As of Terraform 0.8, it has a built-in support for Vault, a secrets management tool from HashiCorp. It's also a big tool, deserving a book of its own. And it's a great solution in order to solve the sensitive data storage problem for Terraform. Consider learning it and using it.

In `Chapter 7`, *Collaborative Infrastructure*, we did not go too deeply into the details of the modern software development workflow. The basics we discussed -- code reviews, working through pull requests -- are just this: basics. There is a number of well-documented workflows that cover many different situations:

- GitHub Flow (`https://guides.github.com/introduction/flow/`): A very simplistic and popular approach
- GitLab Flow (`https://docs.gitlab.com/ee/workflow/gitlab_flow.html`): A slightly different process from the GitLab team
- GitFlow (`http://nvie.com/posts/a-successful-git-branching-model/`): The most complex and an extremely popular model of development as well

All of them are based on Git, though you can achieve similar results with other distributed VCS as well (Mercurial, for example). It doesn't matter much which one you pick in the end, if you follow your chosen one exactly the way it is described. It is important to have a process in place and, as long as you have one, it's already better than Wild West or force pushing to master.

On the continuous integration side of things, it is also important to get to know the whole concept a bit better. There are a number of books and videos from *ThoughtWorks*, who also popularized the whole CI/CD idea. You can find them at `https://www.thoughtworks.com/continuous-integration`.

If you don't want to use GitLab CI, you don't have to (of course). If you seek the same functionality and ease of use as GitHub, then consider one of the many SaaS tools out there: Travis CI, Circle CI, Drone, and others. If you would like to keep your infrastructure pipelines internal, then you can use many hosted tools, including Jenkins, which has great pipelines support:

- `https://www.thoughtworks.com/continuous-integration%20and%20a%20Terraform%20plugin`
- `https://wiki.jenkins-ci.org/display/JENKINS/Terraform+Plugin`

Again, in the end, it does not really matter which CI tool you pick, but it is important that you use one for your infrastructure operations as well.

The many tools around Terraform

Terraform is a small tool. While reading this book, you've hopefully noted how many different other tools were introduced throughout. They are as follows:

- Chef, Ansible, and Puppet: For configuration management
- Inspec and Test Kitchen: For testing
- Terragrunt and Terraforming: As a helper for Terraform operations
- Git, git-crypt, GitLab, and GitLab CI: For teamwork
- S3 and Consul: For storage
- Bash and Ruby: For scripting

You have to learn all of these (or their analogues) to make Terraform production ready. The focus of all HashiCorp tools is to solve one problem and solve it well, and leave everything else to the other software out there.

It can be beneficial quite often - you are not forced to change your toolset; you can pretty much naturally integrate Terraform into your workflows without any big sacrifices. Introducing Terraform to an existing environment is easy. Pick one particular service you want to manage with it and write your first template. Decide on how you want to store your `state` file and roll out upgrades early. Slowly extend the area managed by Terraform. There is no big switch, no big rewrite.

This focus on *one-tool-for-the-job* has some downsides as well, especially if you compare them with competitors. Let's take **CloudFormation**. It is a nightmare to write huge CloudFormation templates. For every small thing, you have to add another 10 lines of JSON or YAML. It is a true example of a bad developer's experience. But note how well it is integrated into the whole AWS ecosystem. And take a look at the AWS Service Catalog: just using CloudFormation, you can offer a complete user-friendly interface for spawning up, updating, and destroying entire stacks, without ever thinking about state files, building this UI yourself, and so on.

Just using CloudFormation and Service Catalog, you could build the whole internal app store for infrastructure environments in a single day. It's the same story for tools such as ManageIQ, which gives you tool not only templating, but the complete life cycle management, full overview of infrastructure, an API to all entities, and a self-service portal for teams inside your organization. If you want to come any close to AWS Service Catalog or ManageIQ with Terraform; you have to do all the work yourself, or pay for Terraform Enterprise, of course, which is a bit of a better alternative than just the Terraform tool itself.

So, keep in mind that Terraform is not a full, packaged solution for your infrastructure. It's a tiny useful tool that must be wrapped with and connected to many other tools if you want to use it at scale and in production.

The rapid development of Terraform

Terraform was first released just a couple of years ago, and it still hasn't reached a major version. It gains more and more in popularity; it grows like crazy, actually, and changes rapidly.

The book you are reading was started with Terraform 0.7.7. It was finished and updated to Terraform 0.8. Even between minor versions, from 0.7.7 up to 0.7.13, there were many small changes that made some code deprecated and some code broken. However, Terraform 0.8 introduced conditionals, as well introducing proper dependencies on modules, which made big chunks of code simply irrelevant now.

With an ever-growing number of contributors and, as a result, the size of the code base, number of providers, and so on, it can be hard to catch up with the latest changes. Keep this in mind when starting to use Terraform: you have to be ready to deal with incompatible changes, with new features appearing, and old ones going away. It is true for every open source project. It is especially true for projects that haven't reached a major version yet, and even more true for such a new and now very popular tool such as Terraform. This brings us to the next point: speculating on the future of Terraform.

Closing thoughts on the future of Terraform

If you invest some effort in a tool and introduce it into a large organization, then you should consider many factors. After all, you don't want this tool to be suddenly abandoned by all developers and have to deal with the expensive process of replacing it. That is unlikely to happen with Terraform though. The company behind it seems to be growing strong, adoption of its tools is growing, and more and more third-party developers contribute their code to Terraform, Consul, Packer, and others. But in which direction will it grow exactly? We can only guess, of course, but let's try anyway.

You have already heard about Puppet -- one of the main configuration management tools out there, backed by a seemingly successful company, Puppet Labs. Unlike Chef, which is pure Ruby, Puppet had its own DSL from the very beginning, which makes it (arguably) easier for administrators to learn when compared with learning a programming language. Today, Puppet language is a bit less DSL and is a bit more of a full language though. In recent releases, it even got a native support for things like loops.

Puppet was made to solve the problem of the automated, predictable configuration of a server. Now, because of the Puppet language itself being powerful, it can be used to configure higher levels of infrastructure, such as AWS resources. As one of the people working at Puppet said (rephrasing):

> *You don't actually care what to manage with Puppet.*

It has a powerful declarative language, with many features, capable of performing updates and being idempotent. Puppet is not just Puppet itself though. It has Hiera to store data, has MCollective for orchestration, and dozens of other tools, either provided by Puppet Labs or by the community (see *The Foreman* (https://www.theforeman.org/) as an example) that make it even better.

Why so many details on Puppet? Because the way it started is very similar to Terraform, and the way it developed over time is similar as well. Terraform has a special DSL instead of a full programming language, and this DSL has characteristics very similar to a Puppet language. It is still a very new DSL, which gets more features over time. Recently, it got simple conditional support, for example. Maybe one day it will even get some kind of loops support in addition to the existing `count` mechanism.

The difference, though, is that, unlike Puppet, Terraform started with the top level of cloud resources instead of an in-server configuration. It appeared just at the right time: when the whole cloud thing exploded. Every major technology company built their own portfolio of cloud services and the need for a tool to manage it properly was really high, and it is even more true today. However, in addition to these cloud providers, Terraform gets more and more providers focused on the software that goes inside your servers. There are, for example, InfluxDB and MySQL providers, being able to create databases on a server. While Puppet went from a lower level of single server configuration to the management of higher layers, Terraform went the other way around -- adding more and more lower-level providers, while still keeping high-level providers up to date.

That's where uncertainty about the direction of Terraform comes from. Is it a tool like CloudFormation, or is it a new-born configuration management tool? Currently, it is neither of these. To be a complete infrastructure provisioner, Terraform currently lacks many important features that are available only in Terraform Enterprise. To be a complete configuration management tool, it lacks so many nice features and the maturity of titans such as Chef and Puppet.

Maybe it will eventually focus on one area, dropping the major support for the other one. Perhaps it will become both a configuration management and infrastructure provisioning tool: the first tool that can successfully take care of all the layers of your infrastructure, from installing packages inside an EC2 instance to creating **Auto Scaling groups** for these instances. But it will be a really long ride (years, for sure) to get there. It will need to have features both from infrastructure provisioners and configuration management tools.

Terraform proved to be useful for putting the cloud under code control, being the best tool for this purpose. It also has some fresh, well-thought ideas that it is built upon.

As the release of version 1.0 is getting closer, we will see if Terraform will become a major player in the configuration management or the infrastructure provisioning market, or whether it will remain a small, focused tool with a very narrow, specific set of applications.

Summary

Now you know Terraform! It would be a shame not to apply this knowledge. Regardless of some concepts about Terraform outlined earlier in this chapter, it's still a great new tool to try and it's extremely useful in many situations. Don't dive into it headfirst; pick a small task, write a template, put it inside a Continuous Integration server, and extend it. IaC is exciting, and Terraform makes it a pleasure to use.

Index

A

Amazon Machine Image (AMI) 75
Amazon Web Services (AWS) 11, 23
  learning 182
AMI Creation with Aminator
  reference link 121
AMI upgrades
  rolling out, with Terraform 127, 129, 130
Ansible
  provisioning with 93, 94
Auto-scaling groups (ASG) 133, 188
AWS CLI
  instance, creating 27
  URL 27
AWS IAM Best Practices
  URL 28
AWS Provider
  configuring 29
  credential file 30
  environment variables 29
  static credentials 29

B

baking images
  with Packer 123, 125, 126
blue-green deployment
  performing 131, 133, 134, 136
builders array definition 123

C

Chef client 95
Chef server 95
Chef
  about 95
  provisioning with 95
ClickOps 11
Collaboration 184
Command Line Interface (CLI) 24
configuration management 15, 183
configuration
  providing, with template_file 76
Consul
  learning 183
  reference link 183
  viewing 84
Content Delivery Network (CDN) 23
Continuous Delivery (CD) 184
Continuous Integration (CI)
  about 184
  reference link 185
counting servers 108, 109, 110, 111, 112

D

data sources
  about 73
  configuration, providing with template_file 76
  configuring 73
  providing, with external_data 80
data
  returning, with outputs 87
dependencies
  controlling, with depends_on parameter 50, 51
  controlling, with ignore_changes parameter 50, 51
dependency graph
  about 41, 44, 45, 46
  reference link 44
directed graph 44
Distributed Denial of Service (DDoS) 108
Domain Specific Language (DSL) 10
dynamic Ansible inventory
  reference link 95

E

EC2 instance
  creating, with Terraform 30
  reference link 31
ECS plus Terraform
  reference link 184
Elastic Compute Cloud (EC2)
  about 23
  instance, creating through Management Console 25
  instance, creating with AWS CLI 27, 28
  using 24
Elastic Load Balancer (ELB) 116

F

files
  uploading, with file provisioner 99, 100
Free Tier 24

G

git-crypt tool
  reference link 149
GitLab
  reference link 146
GraphViz packages
  reference link 46

H

HashiCorp Configuration Language (HCL)
  about 29
  URL 29
highly availability (HA)
  about 113
  creating 114

I

idempotency 9
image baking 75
immutable infrastructure
  about 18, 75, 120, 122, 183
  reference link 183
Infrastructure as Code (IaC)
  about 7, 8, 181
  declarative, versus procedural tools 9, 11
  in cloud 11, 12
  need for 7
  replacements 181
  updates, moving to CI pipeline 167, 169, 172, 174
infrastructure provisioner
  CloudFormation 16
  CloudHeat 16
  configuration management tool 15
  dependency resolution 13
  ease of extension 14
  idempotency 13
  platform agnosticism 14
  requisites 12
  robust integration with 13
  scripting tool 15
  services 13
  smart update management 14
  Terraform 16
  tools, existing 14
infrastructure
  destroying, with Terraform 38
  refreshing 137
Inspec
  servers, testing with 88, 91
  URL 89

L

list variables
  using 67
load balancing 116, 117, 118, 119, 120
local-exec
  provisioning with 93, 94

M

machines
  reprovisioning, with null_resource 101
Management Console
  instance, creating 25
map variables
  using 65
module data
  retrieving, with outputs 60
modules
  about 54

configuring 57
duplication, removing with 54
storing 161, 162

N

Netflix
  reference link 23
null_resource
  machines, reprovisioning with 101

P

Packer, versions
  reference link 123
Packer
  baking images, with 123
providers 22
provisioners 92
provisioning 183
Puppet
  provisioning with 97, 99

R

Relational Database Service (RDS) 157
remote state
  about 151
  connecting 156, 159, 161
remote-exec
  provisioning with 97, 99
resource updates
  handling 36
resources
  importing 138, 139
root module
  about 57, 64
  outputs, using 61

S

scripting tool 15
secrets
  protecting, in Git repository 148
Security Groups (SGs) 15, 27
servers
  testing, with Inspec 88, 91
Simple Queue Service (SQS) 23, 133

Simple Storage Service (S3) 23, 151
simulating conditional 116, 117, 118, 119, 120
Software as a Service (SaaS) 8
StackOverflow
  about 122
  reference link 123
state file
  locking, with Terragrunt 163, 166
  storing 151, 154, 155
  working, with 33

T

template
  creating 53, 54
  moving, to Git repository 146
Terraform Enterprise 20
terraform environment variables
  using 71
Terraform graph
  playing with 46, 47
Terraform Oops 157
Terraform Plugin
  reference link 185
terraform-comunity-modules
  reference link 56
terraform-provider-kubernetes
  references 103
terraform-provisioner-ansible
  reference link 104
Terraform
  about 16, 21
  AMI upgrades, rolling out with 127, 128, 129, 130
  compiling 182
  configuration resources, exploring 82
  development 186
  EC2 instance, creating 30
  modules, integration testing 175, 178
  overview 16, 17, 187
  references 21
  replacements 182
  tools 185
  work environment, preparing 21
terraforming
  reference link 139

Terragrunt
  about 163
  reference link 163
  state file, locking with 163, 166
terrahelp binary
  reference link 148
TerrorFarm 175
TestKitchen tool 175
third-party plugins
  using 103

V

variable files
  using 72

variables
  about 63
  inline, supplying 70
  list variables, used 67
  map variables, used 65
  terraform environment variables, used 71
  variable files, used 72
Version Control System (VCS)
  about 144
  with Git 101 144
Virtual Private Cloud (VPC)
  about 42
  creating 42
VPC Peering 73

Printed in Great Britain
by Amazon